Peter Scott

— some ideas
for the Business
Centre !

Regards

Tim Samuel

Delighting Customers

Delighting Customers

How to build a customer-driven organization

Peter Donovan
Customer Satisfaction Manager
Northern Telecom Europe Ltd.

Timothy Samler
General Manager, Customer Satisfaction
Oracle Corporation UK Ltd.

CHAPMAN & HALL

London · Glasgow · Weinheim · New York · Tokyo · Melbourne · Madras

Published by Chapman & Hall, 2–6 Boundary Row, London SE1 8HN, UK

Chapman & Hall, 2–6 Boundary Row, London SE1 8HN, UK

Blackie Academic & Professional, Wester Cleddens Road, Bishopbriggs, Glasgow G64 2NZ, UK

Chapman & Hall GmbH, Pappelallee 3, 69469 Weinheim, Germany

Chapman & Hall USA, One Penn Plaza, 41st Floor, New York NY 10119, USA

Chapman & Hall Japan, ITP-Japan, Kyowa Building, 3F, 2-2-1 Hirakawacho, Chiyoda-ku, Tokyo 102, Japan

Chapman & Hall Australia, Thomas Nelson Australia, 102 Dodds Street, South Melbourne, Victoria 3205, Australia

Chapman & Hall India, R. Seshadri, 32 Second Main Road, CIT East, Madras 600 035, India

First edition 1994

© 1994 Peter Donovan and Timothy Samler

Produced by Technical Communications (Publishing) Ltd.

Typeset in 10.5 on 12.5pt Times by Fleetlines Ltd, Southend-on-Sea, UK

Printed in England by Clays Ltd, St Ives, plc

ISBN 0 412 61010 8

A catalogue record for this book is available from the British Library

∞ Printed on permanent acid-free text paper, manufactured in accordance with ANSI/NISO Z39.48-1992 and ANSI/NISO Z39.48-1984 (Permanence of Paper).

We dedicate this book to our children:
Gavin, Julian and Matthew.

'Come to the edge,' he said.
They said, 'We are afraid.'
'Come to the edge,' he said.
And they came.
And he pushed them over.
And they flew.

Guillaume Appolinaire

Contents

Foreword

Our two organizations, Northern Telecom Europe Limited and Oracle Corporation UK Limited, share a number of things in common. Both are striving to become world class in markets where technology is moving fast and market change is moving even faster. Both are responding urgently to the challenge of meeting the current requirements – and anticipating the future needs – of customers at the international, national and local level.

We both recognize that customer and employee satisfaction now rank with market share as measures for business success. We accept that there are clear links between delighted customers and profitability, customer loyalty and long-term survival. We are committed to achieving excellence, both as business partners and as employers.

There is already strong co-operation between the growing number of professionals in this field as they work together and exchange experiences for benchmarking and best practice studies. In this spirit of collaboration, we have encouraged Peter Donovan and Timothy Samler to share some of our early experiences with our customer-driven programmes and to stimulate further debate.

Their book provides a wealth of guidance for any organization that has set its sights on delighting its customers and becoming customer-driven. The **ten step approach to delighting customers** breaks new ground and offers a blueprint for others to follow. It exemplifies the practical approach that is taken throughout the book.

The road to customer delight is not an easy one. We hope that this book will provide encouragement for those starting out and give renewed confidence to those already on the journey.

Ian Craig
President and CEO
Northern Telecom Europe Ltd

Mike Harrison
Managing Director
Oracle Corporation UK Ltd

Preface

Business has probably never been tougher. For the first time for many organizations and many managers, survival has become a boardroom issue. Even glamorous sectors like IT (information technology) and financial services have found life uncomfortable.

Faced with this new world of ever-tighter trading conditions, it became the vogue to promote customer commitment and dedication to market needs. For some organizations this trendy 'competitive edge' was clearly no more than skin deep. For others, the customer has genuinely become the driving force of the business.

Achieving this turnaround almost invariably mixes pain and pleasure. We have certainly experienced both in equal measure within our own organizations. The pain has come from taking tough decisions: the pleasure from being part of a change in culture and from working with people with the vision to make things happen.

For both of us, *Delighting Customers* has long been an interest. Now, it borders on a passion. As the customer-driven programmes in our two organizations continue the journey to maturity, we have become aware that we have learned lessons that could be shared. Above all, we felt that there was a need for a basic and practical guide to *Delighting Customers* and to building a customer-driven organization.

Working together, we developed the **ten step approach to delighting customers**. We began to write articles, started to become involved actively with the European Foundation for Quality Management, and took to the hustings at seminars and conferences. Then came the approach from our publishers, Chapman and Hall, and the invitation to write a 'How to' book that would fill a gap in today's market place.

Throughout the process, we have been given generous support from Northern Telecom and Oracle. Particular encouragement has come from Ian Craig and Tony Tuxford at Northern Telecom Europe and from Mike Harrison and Don Taylor at Oracle Corporation. There has been further generous support from an international network of business contacts, many of them working in our field.

Our book is different in three ways.

1. It concentrates on delighting – rather than simply satisfying – customers.
2. It is written for organizations in the business-to-business environment.
3. It is all about **how** to do it.

Business-to-business is the market we both work in and know best. It has also been neglected, with most attention until now focused on consumer services.

In preparing this book, we kept in mind the particular needs of executives and services in business-to-business markets, from high technology and manufacturing through to financial services. The practical content will be as relevant to sales, service, marketing, human resources and quality professionals as to customer satisfaction practitioners and others involved in business process re-engineering, benchmarking and the management of change.

The book has been designed to help you work through each step of a customer-driven programme. Currently, most businesses expend the majority of their customer relations effort on fire fighting rather than on efforts for delighting customers. Our aim is to help you to redress the balance. But until the basics have been mastered, turning the current situation on its head is well beyond the reach of most organizations.

The Appendices (A–I) of the book provide a helpful companion to using the **ten step approach to delighting customers** which is discussed in Chapters 4–8. It reflects the expertise of the world leaders in this field in the form of plans and templates which represent our view of best practice in the implementation of programmes designed to delight customers.

This book introduces some new concepts, such as **the service plane model**, which help to break down the significant task of building a customer-driven organization into manageable chunks.

Most important of all, we provide a comprehensive yet easy-to-follow guide. Whatever your role, this book will determine the next step you will wish to take towards *Delighting Customers*.

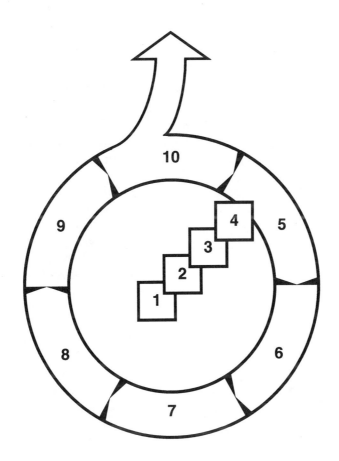

Getting started

Step 1   Setting the service vision
Step 2   Gaining commitment
Step 3   The go/no go decision

Measuring what is important to customers

Step 4   Segmenting the customer base
Step 5   Defining the success criteria
Step 6   Customer feedback systems

Delighting customers

Step 7   Analysing results
Step 8   Making change happen
Step 9   Communicating the changes

Quo vadis?

Step 10 Choosing where next to
         compete

The **ten step approach** to *Delighting Customers*.

Acknowledgements

During the preparation of this book we have accumulated numerous debts of gratitude to the many people around the world who offered encouragement, contributed advice and opinions, or generously shared their experiences with us. In particular, we wish to thank the following key individual and corporate contributors, without whose assistance we could not have reflected current best practice in the art of *Delighting Customers*.

- British Airways: Charles Weiser
- British Telecom: Alan Underwood
- Business Futures Networks, London: Geoffrey Woodling
- European Foundation for Quality Managment (EFQM), Brussels: Geoff Carter
- Forum Corporation, Boston and London: James Blankenship, Dr Paul Burr, Bill Fonvielle and Jennifer Potter-Brotman
- The Harris Research Centre, London: Tom Simpson and Derek Carpenter
- IBM, UK: Barry Ennever, John Rowsell and Barry Povey
- ICL, Europe: David Birch and Michael Tucker
- Jacques Horovitz Institute/MSR, Paris: Jacques Horovitz and Sabine Emad
- KPMG Management Consulting: Sharon Studer
- Northern Telecom Europe: Ian Craig, Dr Tony Tuxford, Mike Jones and Sarah Cundell
- Oracle Corporation UK: Mike Harrison and Don Taylor
- The Performance Group, Oslo: Osvald Bjelland
- The Prudential Insurance Co. of America: Betsy Scarcelli, Robert Methelis and Fred Ingram

In addition, we wish to thank numerous people and organizations for the actions, views and opinions which helped to shape the book. They include:

- Allan Crowley and Associates, Canada
- British Quality Foundation: Malcolm Franks
- Canadian Utilities: Ted Barnicoat
- Citibank, New York: Paul Garber
- Dynamique Satisfaction Client, Paris: Alain Collas
- ED TEL Corporation, Canada: Barry Baptie
- Galgano and Associates, Italy: Maurizio Olivieri
- KPMG Management Consulting: Sharon Studer
- 3M, Europe: Peter Pring
- Mercury Communications Ltd, UK: Keith Ingle
- Price Waterhouse, London: Glen Peters
- The Prudential Assurance Company Ltd, UK: Allan Wright
- Rank Xerox, Europe: Bob Horastead
- Royal Mail, UK: Tim Crew and Brian Lawrence
- Trustee Savings Bank, UK: Wally Welling

We would also like to pay special tributes to Jean Donovan, Paul Burrin of Oracle, Teresa Hall of Nothern Telecom and Barry White of Landmark Corporate Communications who helped us to bring it all together.

Finally, we offer a thank you to the many other practitioners with whom we have talked over the years. You helped us to shape our ideas and gave us the confidence to challenge the norm and find better ways to make the customer-driven programmes happen in our respective companies.

Peter Donovan and Timothy Samler

Section One

The key issues

Chapter 1

What is missing today?

THE KEY MESSAGES . . .

- In a future of unknowns, the need to attract and retain customers is one of the reliable constants in business.

- There is often a disconnection between those responsible for capturing the voice of customers and those people and processes that drive day-to-day business.

- Organizations must deliver high quality customer service at the lowest service plane before proceeding to the next.

- Success comes through getting a lot of things right in combination. It is vital to get the right mix of values, processes and infrastructure to suit the business.

- The concepts are well established.

- Talk is cheap. Implementation, not strategy is key to *Delighting Customers*.

Business leaders today are faced with the relentless pressures of increasing competition, technology, new product innovation and financial performance. In order to be successful senior executives must lead, nurture and navigate their business organizations to cope with the many changes taking place. In this frantic drive for commercial success there is one constant, apart from change itself – the customer. The long-term success of an organization will be determined largely by its ability to differentiate itself in the eyes of its customers: in short, to be **customer-driven.**

A FOCUS FOR SURVIVAL

Many hitherto successful organizations are facing the need to change fundamentally the way in which they operate. Even industry giants can feel the cold. As IBM and Digital can attest, no business is immune. Jim Kearns of DuPont sums it up in this cautionary note.

> Madness is doing what you have always been doing and expecting different results.

As specialists in this field we have seen many large organizations struggling with the same problems as they endeavour to become customer-driven. Some are making progress much faster than others.

What separates the winners from the losers? In our view the difference lies in two simple truths.

- First, honesty and integrity. Successful organizations are brutally honest with themselves and their customers as they grasp the nettle of change. In other organizations the right words are spoken but short-term pressures and personal interests are paramount, serving as implacable barriers to change.
- Second, even organizations with the best will in the world are stumbling over **how** to effect change. They are uncertain where to start, where best to invest their energies and how practically to measure the benefits of their *Delighting Customers* programmes. Successful organisations have significantly moved on from this phase.

THE MISSING ELEMENTS

As real-world practitioners, we have observed a number of deficiencies in this field.

- Most of the available information focuses on broad principles rather than the process of implementation. Experience of *Delighting Customers* shows that implementation of such programmes is not a text book exercise, nor simply a matter of training. It is part of the complex art of leadership and success requires precise management processes.

- Business-to-business services have received relatively little attention from authors in this field. The classic case studies cited in books and articles include consumer services such as McDonald's, Domino Pizza, Federal Express, Marriott Hotels and Disney Theme Parks. Just as most attention has focused on the delivery of consumer items such as hamburgers, parcels and hotel rooms, most of the best examples are drawn from North America. Such examples are instructive and relevant for retail-type service businesses. They are less useful, however, for business-to-business services in areas such as high technology, corporate banking, insurance and finance, and much of manufacturing.

- Best practice studies reveal that the outputs of customer feedback systems, where they exist, have not been integrated fully into the fabric of business organizations. Often there is a weak link, in some cases a disconnection, between the actions of 'information gathering' and 'actions for improvement'; between those responsible for capturing the voice of the customers and those people and processes that drive day-to-day business operations. This problem is further compounded by staff turnover and poor linkages to training programmes. While these organizational weaknesses do not deter the natural champions, the uncommitted majority can use them as an excuse for inaction. If organizations are not actively learning and applying solutions from an integrated customer feedback system, they will never have the factual data to convince the uncommitted to move forward.

We concluded that there is a need to address in greater detail the provision of complex business-to-business service transactions taking place world-wide. Consequently, in this book we focus on the practical issues to be confronted in introducing a *Delighting Customers* programme and creating a customer-driven organization. We present our view on overcoming the key implementation issues and the essential steps in the development and implementation of a programme to delight customers. These are outlined below in the **ten step approach to delighting customers** (see Figure 1.1) and are discussed in detail in Chapters 4 to 8.

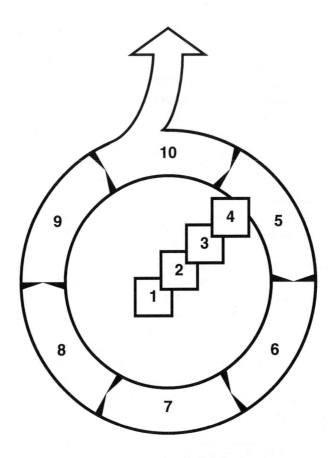

Getting started

Step 1   Setting the service vision
Step 2   Gaining commitment
Step 3   The go/no go decision

Measuring what is important to customers

Step 4   Segmenting the customer base
Step 5   Defining the success criteria
Step 6   Customer feedback systems

Delighting customers

Step 7   Analysing results
Step 8   Making change happen
Step 9   Communicating the changes

Quo vadis?

Step 10   Choosing where next to
           compete

Figure 1.1 The ten step approach to *Delighting Customers*.

WHAT SERVICE BUSINESS IS THE ORGANIZATION IN?

Before starting out on a customer-driven programme, it is important to understand and define the value, or service proposition, that the organization presents to existing and prospective customers. Is it providing a timely, reliable commodity service at a good price? A bank may provide a corporate customer with chequeing, line of credit and payroll facilities. In this case, the service equation will focus on investments in technology and low cost processes. Alternatively, if it is providing business advice in the form of investment counselling and treasury management facilities, the staff will need to combine a greater understanding of the customer's business with expertise in risk management and investment.

When an organization embarks on a programme to improve the services offered there is no turning back. Customer and employee expectations will be raised and failure to deliver will do more harm than good. In fact, customer satisfaction can be damaged by promising improved levels of service that the organization cannot deliver. It is essential that the chosen service propositions are carefully aligned with the willingness and capability of the organization.

This presents two practical questions.

- What is the migration plan for moving from where the organization is today to where it needs to be?
- How will the plan be implemented without raising customers' and employees' expectations too far or too soon?

The risk here is that the organization will be offering an improved service level that it has not yet learned to deliver.

The management team must decide on which service business the organization is currently in, where they want the focus of the organization to be, and the stages they expect to go through to reach their goal. This exercise defines the chosen set of **service planes**. Each service plane defines how 'service offerings' are positioned in the market, the type of services to deliver and its worth to customers. As an example, let us look at the business-to-business services of a high tech company (see Figure 1.2). How can such a supplier, currently offering technology products, position itself to achieve its goal of delivering total business solutions?

In this example, to develop successful business partnerships, the organization's focus must be on delivering high quality customer service at the lower planes before proceeding to the next. There is no point in setting out to fill a leaking bucket without a programme in place to fix the holes.

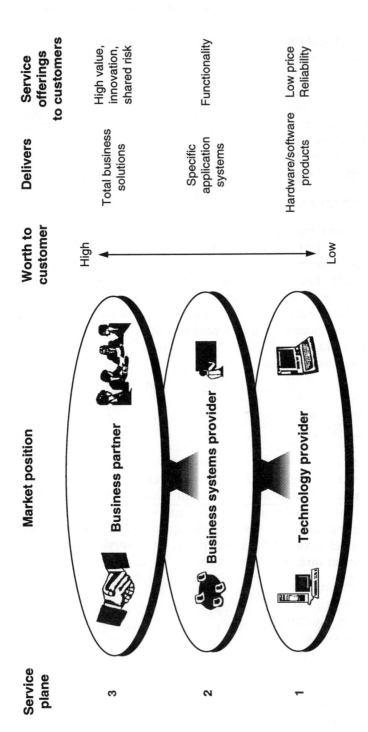

Figure 1.2 An example of the service plane concept: a high technology supplier.

Once the organization has control of the 'service delivery' at one plane it can either continue at this level, focusing on efficiencies and service improvements, or gain market competitiveness by stepping up to the next service plane and a higher set of service propositions. We cover this area in more detail in Chapters 4 and 8.

Maybe some services are already being delivered at a higher service plane than that of the core of the organization. If this is the case then the lessons learned at the higher planes will be invaluable when moving the core of the organization to the next service plane.

WHERE SHOULD MANAGEMENT FOCUS ITS ATTENTION?

Before considering the details and practicalities of implementing a programme to delight customers there are a number of broader organizational concerns that need to be addressed. Implementation typically involves fundamental changes to the organization and, inevitably, this will drive business process re-engineering and continuous process improvement. It also involves the painstaking management of organizational change. Without these vital developments, the odds are stacked higher against a successful outcome for a *Delighting Customers* programme.

Consequently, it is important to understand where management intervention will be most effective and which are the most powerful levers of change. There is no single, simple solution when it comes to implementing a *Delighting Customers* programme. A training programme, a quality process or pious speeches may be important. Alone, they will not be enough. There is no 'Silver Bullet'. Success will come only from getting a lot of things right in combination. It is vital to strike the right balance in developing an integrated, coherent programme.

What are the key ingredients for delivering high quality 'service offerings' appropriate for the chosen market? They all involve influencing the behaviour of people inside and outside the organization, and they fall under three main headings:

1. **values** – including the passion, soul and culture of the organization, within which 'inspirational' leadership plays a key role;
2. **infrastructure** – including the organization's assets and management processes such as information systems, buildings, employee compensation schemes, training and development, and recruitment procedures;
3. **processes** – customer-facing processes including product and service delivery, new product introduction, known best practices and business process re-engineering. These also embrace the quality

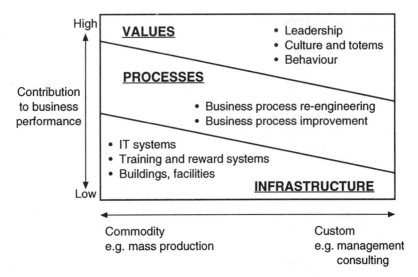

Figure 1.3 VIP model – getting the balance right.

benchmarks of ISO 9000 and the total quality management (TQM) model and self-assessment process developed by the European Foundation for Quality Management.

We find this a useful model for management to assess quickly, and in broad terms, which of these areas will require most attention in their type of business.

As Figure 1.3 shows, the appropriate balance between values, infrastructure and processes (VIP) will vary from organization to organization. Generally, the closer the organization is to a mass production style of operation, the higher the relative importance of infrastructure investment. For example, an automotive factory will invest heavily in production capabilities such as manufacturing equipment, robotics, and research and development (R&D). Such an operation will create a structured physical environment which drives the behaviour and relationships of employees.

At the other extreme, the individuals in a management consulting company have a high degree of task uncertainty in a rapidly changing daily work environment. To influence employee behaviour in this organizational context requires more emphasis on the softer elements such as culture and compensation schemes. The recruitment of people with appropriate attitudes to customer service and teamwork is also a critical factor for success.

IMPLEMENTATION IS KEY

The principles of satisfying – and delighting – customers are already well understood. There are numerous books on the subject; much research has been conducted and there are many experienced consultants in the field. As practitioners in this area though, we have not encountered any fundamentally new ideas in the last five years. Indeed *Delighting Customers* has become a relatively mature school of thought as evidenced by the available material such as articles, conferences, seminars and training courses.

There is no shortage of initiatives. The main constraints to progress are clearly organizational and human. The key question facing business executives today is not What? or Why? customer delight, but How do we make it happen? Implementation, not strategy, is the key to success.

In our view, the top three implementation issues centre on the amount of leadership effort required, the impact of the organization's existing culture and simply knowing where to start. We address these issues in greater detail in the next chapter.

Chapter 2

The implementation issues

THE KEY MESSAGES . . .

- There is no single, simple solution to *Delighting Customers*.

- Success requires inspirational leadership.

- The attitude of an organization is the key predictor of success or failure.

- Successful *Delighting Customers* programmes require a fundamental realignment of the organization towards its customers.

Effective implementation is the key determinant of success for customer-driven programmes. Most companies find this the most difficult part of the process. For example, even the best customer feedback systems will be worthless if the organization cannot drive customer improvements.

In our opinion the key issues for implementation are:

- the vast amount of leadership effort required,
- the difficulty of changing organizational culture, and
- knowing where and how to start.

We will now explore each of these issues in turn, looking at the solutions and drawing on relevant business examples for support.

THE LEADERSHIP EFFORT REQUIRED

Leadership is the key differentiator between those companies, business units, departments and account teams that have made customer-driven programmes happen and those that have not.

There may be other differences, such as available budget, resources, complexity of customer requirements, market expectations or cultural differences. But those companies in the same circumstances with the right leaders will overcome or work around these issues. It is important to get a lot of other things right as well but, in our experience, a *Delighting Customers* programme will not succeed without strong leadership. When the talking is over and it is time to make it happen, leadership is *the* 'critical success factor'. This simple truth emerges time after time when we discuss with other practitioners the source of success and root cause of failure. Quite simply, without pro-active ownership by the organizational leaders, customer-driven programmes are doomed from the outset.

We find that inspirational leadership has a phenomenal effect on driving up customer satisfaction levels. The leadership effort required to satisfy – and then delight – customers takes an inordinate amount of time and effort. But it is a responsibility that cannot be delegated. It is up to the leaders to be the role models.

Executives, department heads and others have very few gaps in their diaries. What time can they spare for *Delighting Customers*? An hour at the monthly meetings? A directive to their managers to 'make it happen'? Pep talks for staff? This is not sufficient. Organizational leaders need to spend *all* of their time in the support of *Delighting Customers* – every day, every meeting, every opportunity. They have to be the main advocates of *Delighting Customers*. They have to set the standards and be the standard bearers.

Assessing leadership effectiveness

Anyone involved in driving an organization's programme for *Delighting Customers* will need to make a formal assessment of all the leaders who are involved at each stage in the life cycle of all the company's products and services. This will generate a debate among senior management to help them understand the importance of their role and the benefits to be gained. Three key questions will need to be asked of each senior manager at every level. (See Figure 2.1.)

- Do they **believe** that *Delighting Customers* is a key business driver?
- Have they made the **time** to lead a *Delighting Customers* programme?
- Do they possess the **skills** to lead a *Delighting Customers* programme?

One point should be awarded for every 'yes', and an extra two bonus points should be given to any leader who is seen as a role model or has already driven up customer satisfaction levels significantly.

This provides an organizational map of roadblocks and drivers. At each leadership level where the points awarded are low, there will be minimal progress and a high resistance to change. Where the scores are high, there should flow innovative and provocative ideas that will help to shake the organization into delighting its customers.

This is not simply a 'one off' activity. *Delighting Customers* programmes are long-term strategies. Leaders come and go, and anyone involved in the implementation of a customer-driven programme will need to update the map regularly and take the appropriate steps to convince the sceptics and support the believers.

Strong leadership at the company and customer/account level (as shown in Figure 2.1) is essential for getting started and delivering early benefits to customers. Without this in place, the other efforts may be wasted. However, to make significant progress beyond the initial phase requires equally strong leadership at the business unit and departmental level to drive through the elimination of the key dissatisfiers and to promote and instigate the development of major customer satisfiers.

Do not be discouraged; customer delight will not happen overnight. It is vital to achieve a critical mass of leadership commitment at the top of the organization before moving down to the next layer of management.

It is the same approach at each management level: make the leadership assessments based on belief, time and skills. Until a manager genuinely believes that *Delighting Customers* is a critical business driver, there is little point in investing a great deal of organizational effort into improvement activities

This is a crucial phase. Fortunately, as we shall see, there are ways of assisting and encouraging the key senior managers to drive the programme.

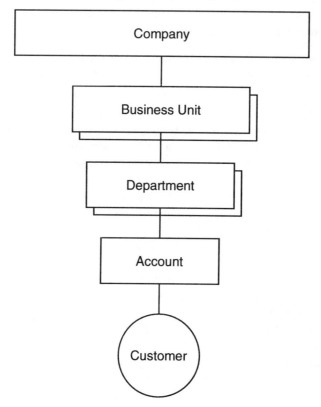

Assessment questions:

• Do they believe that delighting customers is a key business driver?

• Have they made the time to lead?

• Do they possess the skills to lead a delighting customers programme?

Yes = Drivers   **No = Roadblocks**

Figure 2.1 Organizational map of roadblocks and drivers.

Do the organization's leaders really believe?

All business leaders will agree readily that *Delighting Customers* is important. However, if the organization's leaders do not view this as one of the major business drivers, there is a serious problem. In our experience, a customer-driven programme can go no further until this question is settled. At this point, all efforts should be focused on resolving this issue with the manager or managers concerned.

First, hard facts will be needed for presenting a case that is relevant to the leaders concerned. There are now many books and articles on customer satisfaction which provide the research and proof of the benefits to be gained from such a programme. We discuss some of these benefits in Chapter 3.

Second, internal and external case studies will be needed to support these findings. In particular, consider the people and the companies that are held in high esteem by this leader. Additionally, if the leader concerned does not have day-to-day contact with customers, it will be helpful to engineer opportunities to spend more time with customers.

Third, ways must be found to expose such individuals to new ways of working. For example, speaking with peers in other companies that are further down the road towards *Delighting Customers* will provide an understanding of the benefits and issues to expect along the way.

Organizations need to be patient to make time for the individuals involved, but there may be a few individuals who will not participate in a customer-driven programme. In such cases, the most sensible alternative is to move these people from their leadership role. Difficult decisions like this will have to be tackled if an organization is deadly serious about *Delighting Customers*.

Have the leaders made time to lead?

It is not good enough just to invest the odd hour or to make customer delight an agenda item at a regular meeting. Nor is it good enough to insist that others make it happen. Organizations need role models. *Delighting Customers* has to be part of everything that leaders do and it has to be seen as the natural way of working.

Organizations can make this happen by creating a structure for the regular review of customer satisfaction at every level of the business. This could be a mandate to raise the subject as the first issue at every management meeting. It could be a clear requirement that customer satisfaction results and improvement programmes are reviewed at every employee communication session. It should go even further, with customer satisfaction targets being included in three-, five- and ten-year business plans and in compensation policies (salaries, bonuses, rewards and recognition schemes). In other words, the need to delight customers should be integrated fully into all the business activities of the organization.

In this way, time will be created for the organization's leaders to debate the issues, to direct the *Delighting Customers* programme, and to act as role models for others in the organization.

Another approach is to find those people within the business that are providing exceptional leadership. Their success should be promoted and they should be encouraged to share this best practice and to help drive it through all areas of the company.

Do the leaders possess the necessary skills?

Even believers who have made the time to lead still need to be **effective** at leading a customer-driven programme. This is not the same as leading other activities. *Delighting Customers* has a softer element. It is affected by perceptions as much as by facts. Many managers are able to lead based on facts but may find it more difficult to understand and acknowledge the impact of perception.

A programme of training may be necessary. Whatever form it takes, it will need to be flexible enough to suit the needs and characters of the leaders concerned. It is not difficult to identify those who are leading effectively and to see how they have driven up customer satisfaction levels. Their performance can be used as best practice and passed on to others.

Another alternative is to run formal training courses. There are many from which to choose, such as those organized by The Forum Corporation and the Tom Peters Group.

Many senior managers within an organization have little direct contact with customers. Bringing them closer to individual customers gives them a personal 'feel' for how customers suffer and what delights them. This experience will help to develop their understanding and skills in leading a *Delighting Customers* programme. Explore the options for them to spend significant time working in the customer's organization or perhaps invite your customers to come and work in your organization.

In the business examples that follow, we look at the results of two studies of leadership. These examples underline how leaders can create the right environment to sustain a successful *Delighting Customers* programme.

The quotation in the first example illustrates the importance that leaders should attach to creating the right 'spirit and desire' within an organization. But what specific leadership behaviours will be required to create this ethos? The second example explores the actions and behaviours appropriate to leadership.

BUSINESS EXAMPLE

The Performance Group, Oslo, Norway

We make no apology for concentrating on the importance of leadership. As a recent study by The Performance Group stressed:

> No organizational system, no thinking machine, has the power of a truly motivated and committed individual.

The Performance Group has undertaken an extensive *World-Class Performance Study* of 40 of the world's most accomplished leaders. What makes this excellent study unique, is that the majority of these 'superior achievers' were drawn from creative fields rather than the world of business – what the Performance Group terms 'international leaders of group activities'. This study is just one element of a major research and development programme being carried out by The Performance Group, which is supported by companies such as Asea Brown Boveri (ABB), Electrolux, Fortune Magazine and Scandinavian Airlines.

In our opinion, the following quotation from the study crystallizes the art of leadership:

> The main thing is to motivate, to try to release the energies and passion in different individuals in order to make them feel free, to create an illusion that they are actually doing what they are doing out of their own desires and not being led by somebody. That is when the best results happen. In the best possible case, the illusion of freedom becomes true. It is free. Everybody wants the same. All of a sudden the structure of one being the leader and the others being the staff ceases to exist. The structure is not important anymore, but the spirit and desire to achieve it.

Source: Esa-Pekka Salonen
Principal Conductor
Los Angeles Philharmonic & Swedish Radio Symphony
Orchestra

BUSINESS EXAMPLE

The Prudential Insurance Co. of America

In 1993 The Prudential Insurance Company of America conducted a comprehensive benchmarking study on Leadership for Continuous Improvement and Customer Driven Performance. The stated purpose of this in-depth study was:

> to identify the actions and behaviours of people in leadership positions that support and reinforce the successful integration of continuous improvement and customer-driven performance into the culture of the organization.

The Prudential study team established a set of selection criteria to ensure that the US organizations chosen were exceptional in their leadership practices. In addition to The Prudential, six large and well-known business organizations participated in the study. They came from the electronics, transportation, financial services and manufacturing sectors.

Formal benchmarking techniques were used and involved a total of 65 in-depth interviews with senior executives and managers. The Prudential study concluded, among other things, that the behaviour of leaders needs to include the following actions.

1. Clearly, continuously and consistently communicate the purpose of the organization's vision and values.
2. Clearly, continuously and consistently communicate the importance and need to achieve a balance between customer satisfaction, employee satisfaction and financial goals.
3. Listen face-to-face and openly to customers, take action on what is heard and assume accountability for addressing concerns.
4. Listen face-to-face and openly to employees at all levels, take action on what is heard and assume responsibility for addressing concerns.
5. Coach, coach, coach.
6. Require and enable the continuous development of self and others.
7. Continuously and consistently [role] model and reinforce

the skills and behaviours learnt in training courses [and other activities].

8. Senior executives should meet face-to-face with their counterparts in other best practice companies.

Subsequently, The Prudential developed implementation plans and objectives for managers as a means of reinforcing the necessary changes in behaviour and management style. Most leadership effort in the context of a customer-driven organization is about changing the culture of the organization to meet the demands of the marketplace.

In addition to the leadership effort required by a relatively small number of individuals, another difficult issue to be tackled will be that of changing the culture of the organization as a whole.

CHANGING ORGANIZATIONAL CULTURE

Changing the culture is an essential part of a *Delighting Customers* programme. It is not something that can be ignored or tackled some time in the future. Nor is it something that can be run in parallel with the programme. It has to be integrated fully. It has to be shaped by the senior management team and supported by the expertise available within human resources and the other functions supporting the programme.

The culture of an organization and the **attitude** of its leaders are key predictors of success or failure. If the culture and attitude are attuned to the acceptance of change, experiment and learning then the organization has the potential to become a winner by becoming customer-driven. If there is fear of change and scepticism about the benefits of focusing on the customer, then even the best efforts in this area will have little impact.

The development of a customer-focused attitude will need the following elements to be put in place:

- a vision for change,
- a stimulus for change, and
- a reward system to sustain change.

Vision for change   The *Delighting Customers* programme must establish and communicate the vision, values and beliefs of the new culture. This provides a picture of what the organization aspires to and how it sees its guiding business principles. These become the signposts for the journey to becoming a customer-driven organization.

A stimulus for change   The stimulation for changing existing attitudes will come from the activities that are put in place to capture the voice of the customer. The analysis of this information along with the organization's vision and goals will provide a powerful catalyst for change.

Innovation, experiment and even failure should be encouraged. Managing a team where initiatives may fail is a frightening concept for those managers that are indoctrinated in the command and control approach. For these managers, training and coaching will be essential.

The real skill of managers comes in using their experience to keep the balance of successes high and the failures low.

A reward system to sustain change   The attitudinal changes required will be those of behaviour rather than intellectual understanding. This makes it imperative to reward the new behaviour patterns and to discourage the old. This will strengthen motivation throughout the organization to look continuously for ways to serve its customers better. For example, individuals can be measured and rewarded against specific improvement initiatives identified as part of the *Delighting Customers* programme.

The culture that the customer sees is the level of **spirit and desire** of every employee to be truly customer-driven.

It is not possible to disguise the culture of an organization. Whenever we purchase or use an organization's product or service, look at contracts or other documents, contact the switchboard, deal with the finance department for payment of bills, meet with senior management, talk to the employees, or read the press and industry journals, we sense the culture of an organization. We know straightaway whether or not it is customer-focused.

Changing culture is not about training people to smile, to answer the phone within three rings, or to accept blindly that the customer is always right. It is about developing people with a passion for the customer, empowering them to be free thinking, and able to gain the trust of the customer. Even on those occasions when the customer is wrong, employees will be capable of handling the situation in such a way that the customer leaves the experience with a satisfactory solution and importantly, an understanding of what he or she has done to cause it.

In our experience, a **customer-driven culture** is developed by carrying out **customer-focused tasks as a matter of routine** and experiencing the benefits to be gained. It is a gradual process of change, but when a business gets there, everybody knows it – including the customers.

In a business-to-business environment this will only be achieved through a **structured approach** to developing a customer-driven organization. (See Chapter 4 – The ten step approach to *Delighting Customers*.) The effect of this will be fundamentally to re-engineer the organization to become customer-driven. Typically, this will include new systems, processes and organizational structures that encourage the desired behaviour and cause a change in the organization's culture.

Leadership and culture are key to the success of a *Delighting Customers* programme. Equally important is knowing where to start.

KNOWING WHERE TO START

Many organizations keen to initiate a customer-driven programme face the difficulty of knowing where to start. Often they will start in the wrong place, perhaps by putting the entire organization through a two-day training event, the benefits of which never become apparent. There is no single, simple solution to setting a *Delighting Customers* programme in place. In fact, successful implementation may require changes to many aspects of the business including, for example, performance measurement, business processes, organization structure, recruitment and communications. Business success comes from getting a lot of things right simultaneously.

How do we get started? First, the senior executive of the enterprise should appoint an individual champion who is accountable for the design, development and implementation of the programme. This individual must be a member of the senior management team, perhaps a vice-president or a director, and must be seen to be independent, fair-minded and highly credible. He or she will need a small number of fellow professionals to form a project team which will be the focus of the programme for *Delighting Customers*.

Next, the organization must set its service vision and assess the gap between where it currently stands and where it aspires to be. This is accomplished by conducting a company-wide diagnostic to understand its strengths and weaknesses. This enables the firm to identify the programme that will be needed to close the gap and to set in place a structure for continuous improvement. There are several world-class diagnostic assessment programmes available which place a heavy focus on customers, for example:

- the European Model for Total Quality Management,
- the USA's Malcolm Baldrige National Quality Award, and
- the KPMG World Class Performance Model.

The assessment is important for two reasons.

1. It is necessary to identify the scope and nature of the specific projects which together form the migration plan. A key element of the migration plan will be the realignment of the company's policies and practices with the newly established service vision.
2. There is the need to understand the investment required and the key sources of resistance to change which may include the culture of the organization or specific individuals in key leadership positions.

In conclusion, an overall approach is required against which the organization can focus its efforts and measure its progress. Success will not happen by itself. Success is based on taking a systematic, comprehensive and disciplined approach through all the phases of a comprehensive programme of change.

We illustrate this point by showing how two companies, Northern Telecom Europe and Oracle, UK, developed a programme of change to close the gap.

The business examples from Northern Telecom Europe and Oracle provide a flavour of the business activities and change programmes – and the investment – required to close the gap.

Before we look at implementation in detail, it is appropriate to review the specific benefits of a successful *Delighting Customers* programme that can be used to justify the investment. In the next chapter we discuss the business advantages that organizations can reasonably expect and how such changes will affect customers, shareholders, business partners, employees and business leaders.

BUSINESS EXAMPLE

Northern Telecom Europe and Oracle UK

As professional practitioners within these two organizations, we have been through all the phases of a *Delighting Customers* programme. We show below examples of the areas undergoing change as a result of our organizational diagnostics. These projects are integrated into an overall strategic business plan to improve customer satisfaction. (This is explained further in Chapter 5, Step 2.)

Northern Telecom Europe

- Customer guarantees
- Strategic account management
- Product communication
- New product introduction
- People and organization development
- Delivery of business solutions
- Documentation

Oracle Corporation UK

- Order fulfilment process
- Relationship (account) management
- Customer survey programme
- Project delivery
- Product quality
- Quick-fix projects

Chapter 3

Becoming world-class – gaining the business edge

THE KEY MESSAGES . . .

- Research shows a strong correlation between increases in delighted customers and increases in sales and profits.

- For most people, *Delighting Customers* is a natural, satisfying experience and drives organizational effectiveness.

- The reputation of an organization as a service leader is a powerful marketing message for winning new business and consolidating existing customer relationships.

For an organization aspiring to become customer-driven, the cost in time, effort and money can be significant. However, there are major business benefits to be gained from the successful implementation of a programme to delight customers which are:

- increased customer loyalty,
- sustained employee productivity,
- improved business performance, and
- a transition from survival to leadership.

Organizations are right to demand these benefits from their *Delighting Customers* programmes. Measures and systems should be put in place to track these benefits in line with the company's efforts to increase customer satisfaction. Metrics are an essential part of the learning process and a powerful driver of cultural change within the business.

CUSTOMER LOYALTY

A loyal customer base virtually guarantees long-term revenue streams, where strong business-to-business relationships are forged. It establishes barriers to competition and can significantly reduce the cost of sale. The implications for profitability, market share and growth are self-evident. In short, customer loyalty and the retention of business are ways to safeguard long-term business survival.

Research by Rank Xerox shows that 'very satisfied' customers are twice as likely to buy from their suppliers again, compared to 'satisfied' customers. Thus organizations should strive to achieve a very high percentage of delighted customers in order to enjoy fully the benefits of customer loyalty.

Research by Forum Corporation in this field reveals some interesting findings which illustrate the value of actively and effectively managing the relationship with key account customers. Forum Corporation conducted a study of 14 major companies in manufacturing and service industries, including business-to-business markets and relationship-oriented consumer markets such as banking. Revealingly, it found that

> almost 70% of the identifiable reasons why customers left typical companies had nothing to do with the product. The prevailing reason for switching was poor quality of service.

This is illustrated in Figure 3.1.

Clearly, if poor service is offered, a company is unlikely to win long-term customer loyalty. As a consequence, the business will be exposed increasingly to its competitors and may need to invest in marketing and other programmes designed to win new customers to

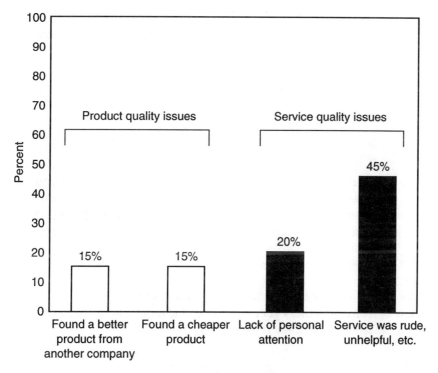

Figure 3.1 Identifiable reasons for switching to a competitor. Totals do not add up to 100% due to rounding. (*Source:* Forum Corporation)

replace those that have been lost. It is a pattern that will need to be repeated until service quality is improved.

The following examples explore the business benefits of customer loyalty.

BUSINESS EXAMPLE

British Airways

British Airways is the world's largest international passenger airline and carries some 28 000 000 customers each year. A key element of its growth strategy is to attract more passengers by investing in top quality service.

British Airways invested significant thought and money in this area and is now reaping the benefits. Part of this investment included the establishment of a pro-active service recovery unit for customers which plays a key role in developing customer loyalty. Charles Weiser, head of this unit observes the following:

> Customer loyalty has improved dramatically. Nearly 80% of correspondents now stay loyal to British Airways thanks to the way their complaint was handled, versus 30% previously . . . World-wide the department's return on investment (money spent to gain repeat business) has leapt to 200%.

In short, British Airways found that for every one pound invested by the Customer Relations Department in customer recovery effort, customers spent two pounds in revenue that otherwise would have been lost through fewer purchases on the airline.

Most companies recognize that one of the secrets of success is to keep their current customers year after year. However, many are struggling with exactly how to make that happen.

BUSINESS EXAMPLE

A chemicals company

A chemicals product company found itself in a very fragmented market with numerous competitors. The number of customers remained the same, but sales were eroding. The nature of the business was such that it would be difficult for the company to differentiate itself through product superiority or price. It decided that service would be the key to success.

Forum Corporation helped the company to conduct preliminary research and convert that information into a questionnaire that could be used with the customer base over the telephone. The overall objective of the project was to determine how to get customers to re-buy at their current level or above, and the questionnaire focused on discovering what was needed to achieve this objective.

The survey uncovered the fact that the customers' decision to re-buy was based on their perception of the company's overall quality. This perception was based on:

- satisfaction with their last transaction,

- an effective customer service function, and
- the demonstration of quality systems and practices.

The information was broken down even further into practices that affected each factor. They then analysed where the largest gaps occurred between customer expectations and their perception of performance. It was determined that if the company improved two practices associated with 'satisfaction with their last transaction', a 14% increase in the bottom line would result.

Employees also play a significant role in building customer loyalty and the introduction of a customer-driven programme will bring with it improvements in employee productivity.

EMPLOYEE PRODUCTIVITY

People like to be winners. The commercial success of the organization in which they work provides a source of pride and a sense of increased job security. Most people want to feel that their contribution is valued by others. This fact is revealed time and again by employee opinion surveys. For example, when Oracle Corporation UK Limited canvassed its employees through meetings, workshops and an employee satisfaction survey, analysis of the results revealed that employees were clamouring for changes to improve service to customers.

The lesson for business leaders is clear. As organizations develop their *Delighting Customers* programmes, harnessing the natural human appeal of satisfying customers can drive up employee productivity significantly.

When British Airways introduced new operating techniques and information technology as part of its drive to increase customer satisfaction, productivity jumped threefold and employee satisfaction rose from the low teens to 69%. As Charles Weiser, head of customer relations, states: 'Rightly, the focus remains on keeping customers happy. . . and it makes us happy to do so.'

A successful *Delighting Customers* programme will build customer loyalty and improve employee productivity. The benefits do not stop there, as we now discuss. It also leads to increases in profitability.

IMPROVED BUSINESS PERFORMANCE

Research indicates that there is a strong correlation between delighted customers and increased sales and profits. To ensure the correct focus and balance in a customer-driven programme, the business leaders should demand improved business performance as a direct result of these efforts. Thus a specific set of measures should be put in place to track the linkage between improved customer satisfaction and business performance.

Typically this set of measures will include:

- customer satisfaction,
- customer loyalty,
- sales, profitability and ROI,
- growth and market share, and
- employee satisfaction.

The Jacques Horovitz Institute, based in Paris, has conducted more than 100 projects in service quality and customer satisfaction since 1987. The Institute has undertaken extensive research of customer satisfaction and has built a database of 63 companies across all sectors of industry in Europe. All studies show a strong correlation between:

- customer satisfaction and sales,
- customer satisfaction and loyalty, and
- customer satisfaction and word of mouth referrals.

This research clearly indicates that an increase in customer satisfaction produces increases in turnover.

An example is provided in the German automotive industry (see Figure 3.2). For many years, one manufacturer's customer satisfaction rating stood around 70%, close to the industry average. As a result of implementing a customer-driven programme, customer satisfaction improved to 80% and turnover by more than 60% from 102 million DM to 165 million DM.

Further evidence is provided by the Profit Impact of Market Strategy (PIMS) database. This includes information on 2,746 business units which has been used to demonstrate how customer-perceived quality drives the bottom-line using PIMS data. Bradley Gale, who was Managing Director of the Strategic Planning Institute in the late 1980s and responsible for running the PIMS database, in his recent book *Managing Customer Value*, illustrates the strong evidence to support this conclusion. Using the customer-perceived quality scores in the PIMS database he concludes that:

- businesses with superior quality average about 30% ROI, businesses with inferior quality average 10% ROI;
- superior quality leads to higher selling prices;
- superior quality doesn't mean higher costs; and
- improving market-perceived quality results in gaining market share at a faster rate than competitors.

Gale comments:

> . . . these new research findings represent powerful evidence that market[customer]-perceived quality drives business results . . . it is closely linked to profitability, price premiums, market share gain, cash flow and market value . . . the evidence shows that practitioners in excellent companies have managed to achieve both [better quality and competitive costs]. This is certainly the goal of world-class, highly competitive companies.

Gale was also involved in the development of the USA's Malcolm Baldrige National Quality Award and influential in demonstrating that quality (customer satisfaction) as perceived by the customer is the most important single long-run determinant of market share and profitability.

It comes as no surprise that out of the seven elements of the

Development of turnover in million DM

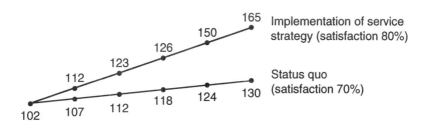

Figure 3.2 An example of customer satisfaction in the automotive industry, Germany. (*Source:* Jacques Horovitz Institute.)

MBNQA, customer satisfaction is given the highest value – 300 points out of 1000. The next highest element is given 180 points. This emphasis is also repeated in the European Quality Award.

As time has gone on, businesses have been able to support this. For example, IBM business units that score over 500 points outperform the average and 'operating profit growth' dramatically outperforms their low-scoring sister businesses. As Gale states in his book, while IBM as a whole may be perceived to be struggling, some parts of the company have learned to make money by serving the customer well.

These examples provided by Horovitz and Gale underline the nature of business benefits that executives should expect as they lead their organizations in the transition to becoming world-class.

A TRANSITION FROM SURVIVAL TO LEADERSHIP

Quite simply there are fewer headaches for executives whose organizations provide world-class service. The time previously required to deal with customer complaints can be invested in leading the organization to world-class performance. Having the reputation as a service leader is a powerful marketing message for winning new business.

As organizations move from survival mode into a leadership role there are many marketing opportunities to help win new business and beat the competition. Companies like Rank Xerox, Hewlett-Packard, ICL and British Airways have exploited the powerful marketing messages of being known as a customer-driven organization in a variety of different ways.

- They have advertisements which underline mastery in service, such as extraordinary service guarantees or the favourable results of independent customer surveys.
- They actively position themselves as a source of best practice.
- They use existing key account customers as references for winning new business.
- They place articles and interviews with CEOs in the newspapers, the trade press and company publications.

Some companies like British Airways and Rank Xerox reached a *crisis point* before setting about building a customer-driven organization. Why wait for a true crisis? 'Inspirational leadership' and the deployment of the voice of the customer throughout the organization can induce a 'crisis mentality' to drive through the necessary changes. Why not make it happen now?

In the next section we discuss the details of **how** to build a customer-driven organization.

Section Two

How to build a customer-driven organization

Chapter 4

How to make it happen

THE KEY MESSAGES . . .

- The people involved in the development of the *Delighting Customers* programmes need to be marketeers and salesmen rather than researchers or inspectors.

- Organizations need a structured approach to build and sustain a customer-driven organization.

- Satisfying customers is a never-ending journey.

SELLING CHANGE

Organizations should treat their *Delighting Customers* programmes as a product, market the information gathered and sell change at all levels. Therefore, to make change happen requires a frame of mind more akin to that of a marketeer or salesman than an inspector or researcher.

As the organization embarks on this programme of change, it will need to sell it hard and sell it continuously. Although we have already discussed examples of employees readily embracing the *Delighting Customers* philosophy once it can be seen to be working, the programme has little momentum of its own in the early stages, and will need a complete marketing strategy which has full budget approval – from a communication plan right down to give-aways and promotional exhibitions for staff and customers.

It will simplify the process if 'internal' customers within the business are segmented into different types: executive, middle management, employees, process owners and so on. For each group, it will be necessary to determine what information is needed, and how it can be generated, communicated and delivered. The 'product' requires packaging so that it meets – or preferably exceeds – needs and expectations. Look for the most convenient and effective formats to make it easy for these internal customers to analyse and use the information.

This marketing approach will help to bring together the many initiatives that are under way in the organization and focus these energies under the banner of delivering real value to customers. It also simplifies the assembly of a team of cross-functional experts to make *Delighting Customers* happen.

With the marketeer's frame of mind, the organization will be able to set a direction and priorities for the programme that are clearly focused on the needs of the customer. To make a customer-driven programme work across the organization requires a systematic approach. We call this the **ten step approach to delighting customers** designed to help the business to become world-class in delighting its customers.

THE TEN STEP APPROACH TO DELIGHTING CUSTOMERS

Organizations need a comprehensive map if they seriously plan to journey down the road of *Delighting Customers* as this typically involves radical change. The **ten step approach** will place any organization firmly in control of the services it is offering. In our experience our approach will provide the organization with the road map to achieve its vision and long-term strategic goals.

We outline this approach in Figure 4.1, which illustrates the ten steps and present below the key questions that organizations must ask themselves along the way.

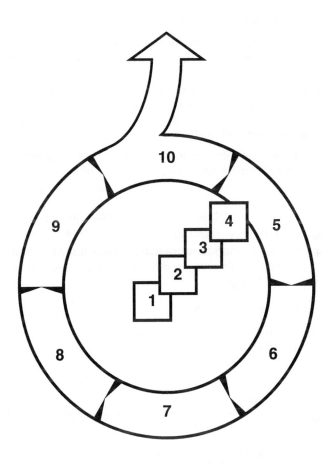

Getting started

Step 1   Setting the service vision
Step 2   Gaining commitment
Step 3   The go/no go decision

Measuring what is important to customers

Step 4   Segmenting the customer base
Step 5   Defining the success criteria
Step 6   Customer feedback systems

Delighting customers

Step 7   Analysing results
Step 8   Making change happen
Step 9   Communicating the changes

Quo vadis?

Step 10 Choosing where next to
         compete

Figure 4.1 The ten step approach.

The key questions to ask

Step 1 – setting the service vision

- What service plane does the business aspire to?
- What makes the organization's service package different from the competition?
- How will the service vision be communicated simply and effectively to customers, employees and business partners?

Step 2 – gaining commitment

- What are the most obvious shortcomings between the service vision and existing business practices?
- What major projects will the organization need to initiate at the outset?
- Who are the key individuals, by name, who will sponsor, facilitate and manage the necessary changes?
- Does the organization have enough people who are committed and have the right skills and experience to overcome the inevitable resistance to change?

Step 3 – the go/no go decision

- What is the overall probability of success?
- What are the risks and benefits associated with each major project?
- Can the organization afford the necessary investment of money and key human resources?
- Does the organization have the will and ability to become customer-driven? If not, stop now.

Step 4 – segmenting the customer base

- What are the particular needs of specific customers in different markets?
- What is the nature and quality of the business relationships with key customers?
- What role does the organization play in the success of its customers?

Step 5 – defining the success criteria

- How will the organization measure the success of the *Delighting Customers* programme in business terms?

- How will the company measure and reward teams and individuals when operating in its chosen service plane?

Step 6 – customer feedback systems

- How can the organization capture the customer's viewpoint most effectively?
- How will the business quantify what is important to customers?
- How important are confidentiality and independence in this process?

Step 7 – analysing results

- How will the results of customer feedback be interpreted and help to build a customer-driven organization?
- Who will analyse the results?
- Who will be responsible for service improvement and evolution?

Step 8 – making change happen

- How will the organization be made to change in response to customer feedback?
- How will continuous service improvement be driven through a combination of quick fixes and long-term organization re-engineering?

Step 9 – communicating the changes

- How will the organization communicate back to customers what they have told the researchers and how the business is responding?
- What will be the impact of this response on customers, employees and business partners?
- How will the loop be closed?
- How will the company decide when is the right time to communicate?

Step 10 – choosing where next to compete

- How can the total product be embellished in order to move qualitatively into the next dimension of service?
- What new investment in skills and infrastructure is required for success in this next, higher service plane or will the business choose to remain on the same service plane?
- If so, where will efforts be focused to enhance existing services and effect process efficiencies?

Although the steps occur in a logical sequence, in practice many of the activities will be undertaken in parallel. This is a never-ending journey and there will be many reiterations within each phase. For example, different products and customer mixes may be at different levels of the service planes as discussed in Chapter 1. With one product, it may be necessary to be no more than an excellent and reliable supplier. For another, the solution may well be to offer a partnership where risks are shared and there are mutual benefits.

For each of these types of service offerings you will need to follow the ten steps that we have outlined, but in each case, implementation will need to be handled differently.

The stage that the business has reached in its evolution towards becoming customer-driven will dictate the starting point on the ten steps. An organization starting out on the journey needs to begin at Step 1 and work through to Step 10. In our experience this will take at least twelve months.

At the end of Step 10, the company will have assessed the overall effectiveness of the programme and be ready to move into the continuous improvement phase. This will require returning to Step 5, reassessing the success criteria and working through to Step 10 again. This continuous improvement cycle will be repeated until the organization identifies the need for a **step change,** involving a move up to the next, higher dimension of service. This is likely to require the use of business process re-engineering techniques.

If the business already has a clearly defined service vision, it can begin with measuring what is important to customers (Steps 4–6). And if a well developed customer feedback system already exists, the company will probably wish to refocus efforts on delighting customers (Steps 7–9).

We have discussed this approach with many of today's best practitioners and each agrees that it contains all the elements needed to develop a truly customer-driven organization. Can any organization afford to be just one of the pack, driven by the demands of customers and competitive pressure? Should not the aim be to emerge as the leader, continuously *Delighting Customers* and gaining the business edge over competitors?

In the following chapters we work through the **ten step approach to delighting customers,** which will enable a customer-driven organization to be created and sustained.

Chapter 5

Getting started

INTRODUCTION

In this chapter we demonstrate how to get started using Steps 1, 2 and 3 of the **ten step approach to delighting customers.**

Step 1: setting the service vision
Step 2: gaining commitment
Step 3: the go/no go decision

These first three steps will be critical to the success of the *Delighting Customers* programme. Steps 1 and 2 must be completed before the go/no go decision is taken in Step 3.

Unless the service vision is practical and easy to communicate, it will be difficult to gain the necessary levels of commitment throughout the organization.

If at any stage there are doubts about the ability of the business to provide customers, employees and business partners with tangible benefits, the organization must hit the brakes. It is essential not to move forward until the company is confident that it can deliver.

STEP 1 – SETTING THE SERVICE VISION

> THE KEY QUESTIONS TO ASK . . .
>
> - What service plane does the business aspire to?
>
> - What makes the organization's service package different from the competition?
>
> - How will the service vision be communicated simply and effectively to customers, employees and business partners?

First of all, let us summarize this step. As discussed in Chapter 1 (see Figure 1.2), business leaders must develop a practical definition of what the organization aspires to. This service vision can be established by:

- deciding what service business the organization is currently in and the future aspirations of the organization;
- assessing how accurately the current business vision, mission, goals and values reflect customers needs and expectations; and
- re-defining the organization's vision to support the future service business to which the organization aspires.

The first task is to initiate a debate to address these issues. For this debate to be effective, it must be conducted honestly and constructively, as there will be major differences between what people say and how they actually behave.

The development and articulation of purpose is all about developing a simple set of words that is readily understood by customers and employees. It conveys what services the organization delivers, and it can be translated readily into operational objectives. It is also about challenging the organizational leaders to commit openly to a vision for the future, including identification of the service planes in which it chooses to compete. In so doing, the leaders will put their reputations on the line.

Let us discuss the requirements of this step in more detail.

Initiating the debate

Key business data will form an integral part of the debate and should include product revenue profiles, market developments and customer expectations. Analysis of this data is essential.

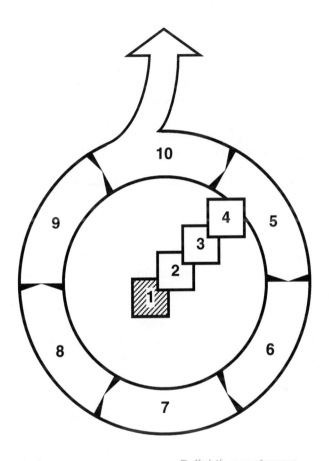

Figure 5.1 Step 1 – setting the service vision.

For example, the dramatic success of Oracle Corporation UK Ltd over a ten-year period was based on the company's ability to win new customers. An assessment of its services revealed that a growing proportion of its revenues were resulting from the sale of technical support, consulting, training and other services to **existing** customers. This realization prompted Oracle to ask fundamental questions about the nature and evolution of the services it provided.

Other data that are required to support a review of this kind will include an understanding of how customers currently feel about existing products and services. Equally important will be an understanding of the nature of current and future competition for each of these product and service areas.

Therefore, the debate must address specifically the question:

What will be the future expectations of customers?

Geoffrey Woodling of the Business Futures Network observes that:

Satisfaction is a notoriously difficult quality to define. It is an individual expression of expectation. No two customers, any more than any two customer competitors, will be directly comparable . . . customers expectations of each competitor will differ. Hence common standards of performance to satisfy yesterday's expectations will no longer differentiate competitors. Only a continuing awareness of tomorrow's expectations will allow suppliers to improve customer satisfaction.

During the debate it is helpful to look at other organizations as a way of introducing new ideas and behavioural forms into the business. A standard feature for all elements of the programme is the requirement to benchmark the critical processes at every step of the way. How other companies operate – particularly competitors and other leaders – can provide a simple set of best practices which can be used to influence and convince others to embrace new ideas and consider new behaviours. This will help to sow the seeds of change and introduce the cultural and behaviour attributes that are expected of a customer-driven business. It will also identify the vision, projects and time-scales set by others and this will be invaluable information for setting realistic and achievable goals.

For the debate to be successful requires bold leadership together with a healthy measure of new ideas and vision from the top. Ultimately, decisions must be made about the shape of the final service vision.

- In which markets or service planes does the business want to compete?
- How will it go about it?
- Where are the gaps between the services being offered now and the future service aims of the company?

The key element in this whole exercise will be the ability of the organization to deal honestly and openly with issues which may go to the heart of the existing culture. It may well involve the slaughter of one or more sacred cows or organizational icons.

What should the service vision look like?

Following this debate, the organization will have developed a vision, mission or statement of its service offerings. Ultimately, the most difficult part of this step is putting the service vision into practice. It must have clear operational imperatives. A practical test for any service vision or service proposition will be to assess its practical relevance for each of the key stakeholders – customers (both internal and external), employees, business partners and the owners of the company. Rather than emphasizing lofty, normative values, it should focus on specifics such as business practices and behaviour, as illustrated in the following practical examples.

BUSINESS EXAMPLE

ICL

At ICL, the company's values are promoted in 'The Four Principles of Customer Care', a down-to-earth statement of 'The ICL Way'.

- Customer care has to be defined as exceeding customer expectations – not merely meeting them.
- The system for customer care is personal service – not just following the process.
- The performance standard is **First Choice Supplier** – not 'We can't win them all'.
- The measurement of customer care is what **the customer** says – not what **we** think it is.

BUSINESS EXAMPLE

ED TEL Corporation

When developing its service vision a few years ago, ED TEL Corporation, a telephone company in western Canada, produced some specific quotations to describe its vision in behavioural terms.

- Customers will say:

  The folks at ED TEL are thoroughly professional, committed to excellence in every detail, and care about me. I get value for money.

- Employees will say:

  I enjoy providing outstanding customer service as part of the ED TEL team. ED TEL treats its employees with respect and integrity, and offers numerous opportunities with challenge and growth. I enjoy my job.

- Owners will say:

  We are proud that ED TEL is a profitable and efficient operation which cares about its customers, its employees and the community it serves.

- Competitors will say:

  ED TEL is a worthy and ethical competitor. We have a great deal of respect for that company.

- Suppliers will say:

  ED TEL is the most innovative telco in Canada and can make things happen in a hurry. ED TEL treats us as a partner in their business.

In another example, the Royal Mail in the UK linked its business mission to the means by which it would be achieved.

BUSINESS EXAMPLE

Royal Mail

Royal Mail sees its business mission in these terms:

> Our mission is to be recognised as the best organization in the world distributing text and packages.

We shall achieve this by:

- excelling in our collection, processing, distribution and delivery arrangements;
- establishing a partnership with our customers to understand, agree and meet their changing requirements;
- operating profitably by efficient services which our customers consider to be value for money;
- creating a work environment which recognizes and rewards the commitment of all employees to customer satisfaction;
- recognizing our responsibilities as part of the social, industrial and commercial life of the country; and
- being forward looking and innovative.

In a further example, the service vision is described through management of expectations against a few key deliverables and the measures used to define success.

BUSINESS EXAMPLE

Oracle Corporation UK

When it comes to organizational values, Oracle sees these in terms of expectations that it seeks to meet. The two categories are:

1. Customer expectations:
   - high quality,
   - affordable price,
   - easy purchasing experience, and
   - life cycle service.

2. Employee expectations:
   - challenging experience,
   - excellent rewards,

- personal development, and
- career growth.

Oracle has quantified what it means to be customer-driven, its long-term success criteria are:

- 95% customer satisfaction
- 95% employee satisfaction
- 95% shareholder satisfaction
- 50% market share

In summary, a service vision needs to capture the essence of the service proposition for the customer, the idea of the service culture that underpins it and also the idea that the service will be differentiated for each particular market place. For example, 'We believe the customer is Number One' is fine but it lacks operational bite. The vision needs to be stated in practical terms to include a flavour of service level guarantees, while also retaining the essence of the vision itself.

Conclusion

The debate should result in a practical and operational description of the service proposition which can be readily communicated to employees, customers and business partners alike. The debate must be based on some quantitative and qualitative assessment of the current situation in terms of current and future customer needs and expectations, revenues and market growth. It should also include discussions and input from all principal customer types. The entire process needs to be honest and open-minded, because the discussions will need to test some of the basic assumptions about existing business practices and modes of operating behaviour. Lastly, it will be important to identify some specific measures of success – a few yardsticks that will tell the business leaders whether they have been successful in attaining the vision. The key deliverable for this step will be a short summary of the service vision. This should specifically address those service planes, discussed in Chapter 1, in which the organization intends to compete.

The service vision should be capable of being communicated in a number of different ways.

- It should be flexible enough to take the form of a video presented by one or more of the senior management team.
- It should form an integral part of the standard messages used for the broad range of corporate marketing materials – from slide

presentations to tender documents, promotional literature to media information packs.
- Above all, the service vision messages must be easy to communicate clearly to customers, employees and business partners, so that they all understand the new direction of the organization.

In our experience this exercise does not usually require fundamental changes to existing business goals and mission statements. In practice, most large businesses have a well-articulated and crafted mission statement. What is required typically is a fine tuning of the existing statements and values to give them real practical and operational meaning for delighting customers across all lines of business.

Now that the service vision has been defined the next step is to assess and quantify in greater detail the variance between the vision and current practice, and to gain the commitment of the organization to close this gap in the move to becoming truly customer-driven.

AT THE END OF THIS STEP . . .

There will be a well-defined service vision expressed in practical, operational terms which can be communicated widely to customers, employees and business partners.

STEP 2 – GAINING COMMITMENT

THE KEY QUESTIONS TO ASK . . .

- What are the most obvious shortcomings between the service vision and existing business practices?

- What major projects will the organization need to initiate at the outset?

- Who are the key individuals, by name, who will sponsor, facilitate and manage the necessary changes?

- Does the organization have enough people who are committed and have the right skills and experience to overcome the inevitable resistance to change?

In this step we will assess the gap between the service vision set in Step 1 and the current behaviours and practices. Using a diagnostic health check, we will identify what needs to be done to close the gap and install a permanent process for driving continuous improvement. This knowledge will enable the business to gain the commitment of those responsible for the areas to be changed. In our experience, this step and further steps will benefit greatly from the **appointment of a senior executive with authority to manage the overall programme.**

The health check should identify a programme of projects designed to address those areas where it is immediately evident that weaknesses exist. There is no need to wait for detailed confirmation from customers before resolving issues where improvement is clearly long overdue. Some of the changes that are necessary may well be unpalatable.

The diagnostic health check, discussed in detail as part of this step, aims to reveal shortcomings that may exist in areas such as:

- existing levels of customer satisfaction and service delivery capabilities which requires interviews and discussions with customers and employees and which will refer to any previous customer surveys carried out;
- employee attitudes and organization culture which will involve workshops and meetings with employees and an assessment of employee attitudes to customer service – (key to this assessment will

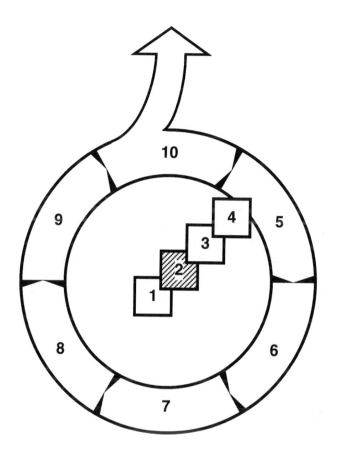

Figure 5.2 Step 2 – gaining commitment.

be an understanding of the organization's willingness and ability to change);

- the impact of the existing organization structure which requires an understanding of how the business unit structure, for example, helps or hinders business performance and which also includes a review of job roles and design; and

- the role of measurement and reward systems and the calibre of recruitment, training, etc. How do existing business practices contribute to encourage appropriate behaviour for individuals and teams?

This step should be completed in less than three to four months. Taking longer means that the initiative will lose momentum and the process will be unnecessarily expensive.

Experience also shows that a great deal of time, likely fascinating for those involved, can be wasted on a descriptive analysis of the issues associated with the current situation. People are naturally tempted to describe, often in laborious detail, what the problems are. Beyond a certain point, such efforts have a minimal value. The business is better served by investing these energies into designing solutions to address the top two or three issues.

This analysis will result in the identification of a number of quick-fix projects of immediate benefit, such as improvements in customer communications, or facilities for customer and employee training. The analysis will also result in the identification of long-term projects that strike at the heart of the problems, at the infrastructure of the enterprise. Examples might include business process re-engineering or large, integrated IT systems that provide the backbone for high-quality service delivery processes.

It may be necessary to restructure the organization and set new measures of success for business units and individuals. Such projects are risky, expensive and time-consuming. Therefore, it is vital to focus on a small number of key projects. As part of this exercise it may be necessary to realign business policies and procedures to support the new vision. Revised compensation schemes may also be needed for the sales force, for instance.

For each key project, the names of individual sponsors and 'doers' must be identified and sufficient resources made available. By the time this step is completed, there must be a critical mass of named individuals who are publicly committed to the changes that have been agreed as part of this overall game plan for significantly improving customer satisfaction. There will also be a commitment from the senior management team to realign the organization's policies and procedures against the vision identified in Step 1 and the organization should be capable of mobilizing hearts and minds behind the vision.

Before we attend to the detail of the core of this step – the diagnostic health check – we should consider the key drivers of business performance.

As discussed in Chapter 2, the diagnostic health check should be based on world-class business criteria, with a heavy focus on delighting customers. Self-assessment against any of the models mentioned below will meet this requirement:

- the European Model for Total Quality Management, developed by the European Foundation for Quality Management (see Figure 5.3),
- the USA's Malcolm Baldrige National Quality Award (MBNQA), and
- the KPMG World Class Performance Model.

In this chapter we have chosen to use the KPMG World Class Performance Model to illustrate the use of a diagnostic check. To provide a comparison with the other diagnostic checks, we have included an extract from the EFQM Guidelines for Identifying and Addressing Business Excellence Issues as shown in Figure 5.4 and the approach using the MBNQA model is similar.

Self-assessment involves the regular and systematic review of the organization's activities and results. According to the EFQM,

> This process allows the organization clearly to discern its strengths and the areas in which improvements can be made. Despite the fact that every organization is unique, the European Model for Total Quality Management model provides a framework for self-assessment that is applicable to every business organization.
>
> Processes are the means by which the organization harnesses and releases the talents of its people to produce results. In other words, the processes and people are the **enablers** which provide the **results**.

(The principle is shown graphically in Figure 5.3.) The EFQM continues:

> The model was developed as a framework for the European Quality Award. Essentially the model tells us that customer satisfaction, people (employee) satisfaction, business results and impact on society are achieved through leadership

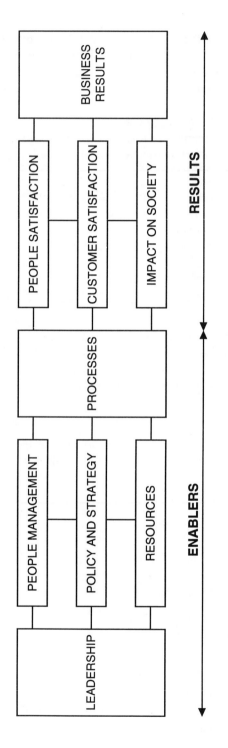

Figure 5.3 EFQM model for Total Quality Management.

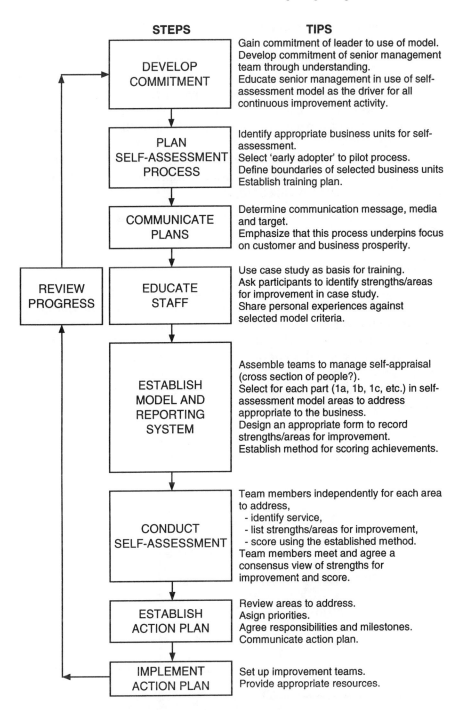

Figure 5.4 EFQM process for self-assessment.

driving policy and strategy, people management, resources and processes.

Each of the nine elements shown in the model is a criterion that can be used to assess the organization's progress towards world-class performance. The results aspects are concerned with what the organization has achieved and is achieving. The enablers aspects are concerned with how the results are being achieved. The objective of a comprehensive self-assessment and self-improvement programme is to review regularly each of these nine criteria and, thereafter, to adopt relevant improvement strategies.

The European Quality Award process for self-assessment is shown in Figure 5.4.

The performance drivers

KPMG Management Consulting has developed a world-class performance model which encourages organizations to ask the right questions and come up with the right answers (see Figure 5.5). What the model shows clearly is that high performance business is designed around customers. This includes not only the overall organizational structures, but also how teams work together and how individual jobs are designed. The model also indicates that there are seven attributes which, taken together, drive high performance.

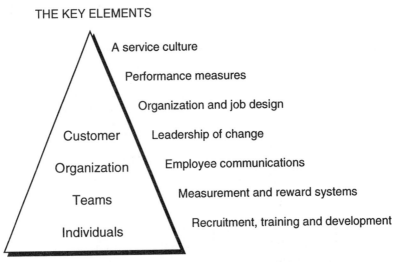

THE KEY ELEMENTS

- A service culture
- Performance measures
- Organization and job design
- Leadership of change
- Employee communications
- Measurement and reward systems
- Recruitment, training and development

Customer
Organization
Teams
Individuals

Figure 5.5 KPMG World Class performance model.

This best practice model illustrates what some companies have focused upon to achieve high performance. First, they have asked tough questions about the effectiveness of the following aspects of their company.

- Their **relationships with customers**
  How do customers perceive the service they receive?
- The fundamental **design of the organization**
  Does it help or hinder performance?
- **Team working**
  How effective is inter-departmental co-operation?
  How do departments and sub units pull together?
  How does the organization work with its business partners and suppliers to the benefit of customers?
- **Individuals**
  How effective are individuals at all levels?
  Do they have the necessary conceptual and technical skills?
  Equally significant is whether or not they have the right attitude?

Second, there are seven typical characteristics, or attributes, of high performing companies:

1. A **service culture**
   Is the organization customer-orientated or introverted?
2. **Performance measures**
   Is there a balanced scorecard of measures used to assess the success of the organization as a whole?
3. **Organization and job design**
   Is the organization engineered around customers and core business processes?
4. **Leadership of change**
   Are there natural leaders in key positions who lead by example?
5. **Employee communications**
   Does the organisation understand that it cannot over-communicate with employees?
6. **Measurement and reward systems**
   Do they exist for teams and individuals?
7. **Recruitment, training and development**
   Is there a commitment to investment in human resources which have been very carefully chosen in the first place?

In our experience, the world-class organizations score highly in all seven of these areas. However, it is also fair to say that, as yet, we have not encountered an organization that scores ten out of ten on each attribute. Even the best organizations in the world have yet to achieve perfection.

We conclude that progress in one area alone will not ensure success. It is a combination of factors, taken together, that will drive business performance and customer satisfaction in the right direction. It is against this model that the organization can undertake the diagnostic health check and the projects that will be identified as a direct result.

The diagnostic health check

This exercise has two principal objectives.

- The first will be to undertake a descriptive analysis of the organization and its customers. The way that we describe the organization will be very much in terms of its culture, its ethos, and the principal operational practices and behaviours.
- The second objective will be to define and capture all the issues which characterize poor service performance. This may expose customer complaints which are universal. All customers may complain about the quality of invoices, for example. Similarly, the review may show that whereas the clear goal of the company is to manage the long-term customer relationships with key accounts, in fact, the compensation schemes and recruitment practices of the business are inconsistent with this aim.

To illustrate the approach for carrying out this diagnostic check process, we use the KPMG DPE (diagnostic–plan–execute) model (Figure 5.6). This detailed diagnostic assessment begins with the customer – the obvious place to start. The requirement is to calibrate and quantify existing levels of service, by line of business, as they are currently perceived by customers. This analysis would typically include:

- reference to any previous customer satisfaction surveys or market studies;
- a mini customer satisfaction survey to provide pointers to current attitudes;
- interviews with major account customers;
- focus group meetings with customers;
- analysis of other data such as customer complaints, calls to service desks or information centres; and
- interviews and workshops with employees at the sharp end who are known to be a mine of information.

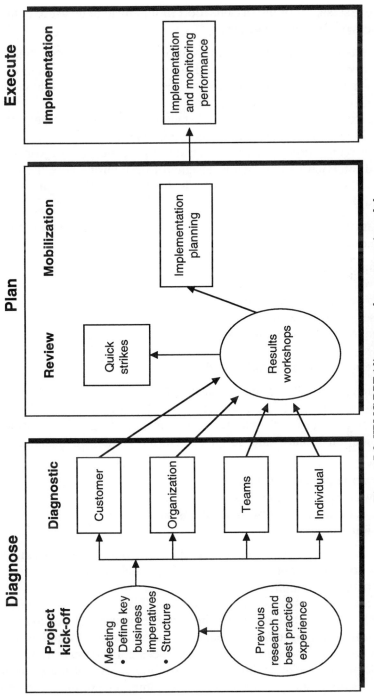

Figure 5.6 KPMG DPE (diagnose–plan–execute) model.

The assessment of the organization should include measurements of business performance, such as:

- simple metrics for key business processes such as profitability or service intervals for external and internal customer performance;
- a review of existing corporate performance measures and how these influence organizational behaviour;
- the extent to which customer satisfaction is an explicit element of the business planning and budgeting process; and
- the organizational culture as measured in, for example, workshops and interviews and which is designed to establish where the power lies, the control systems, the rituals, the routines, the cultural totems and the icons.

Teams and individuals will be assessed through a combination of techniques which can include:

- employee attitude surveys,
- psychometric profiling and assessment centres,
- job design and qualifications,
- assessment of recruitment and training processes, and
- employee turnover and absenteeism.

The results of the diagnostic health check

The diagnostic will identify disparities between what the organization wishes to accomplish in service terms and the current state of affairs. A number of issues will emerge. First, closing the gap will require a combination of 'hard' and 'soft' fixes. Hard remedies will include:

- new IT systems,
- new buildings and facilities,
- new compensation schemes,
- measurements and rewards systems, and
- training programmes.

On the soft side there will be a number of organization issues that will relate to how people think, believe and behave, e.g. the role of leadership by example.

The second issue is the importance of education and training. Employees must understand the importance of satisfied customers and the business implications of what customers currently complain about and, indeed, what delights them. Some specific skills may be required to enable better relationships with customers. A business partner relationship implies a range of skills including, for example, the ability to listen, empathize and communicate in business terms.

Thirdly, the sources of resistance to change will be identified in the issue of fundamental beliefs and values which are at the heart of the organization's culture and style. In our experience, where major change is required, changes in personnel will be inevitable. This is a nettle which must be grasped. For example, a senior manager who has been around for many years but who has a 'customer-last' mentality must be moved if a customer-driven programme is to be taken seriously. Left in place, such individuals will symbolize to the rest of the organization that talk is cheap.

Gordon Williams, chief executive officer at Vought Aircraft, USA, underlines this point.

> Middle management is not the problem. They resist change because they believe upper management doesn't really believe it.

For this reason, it is vital to enlist the support of a critical mass of supporters in the organization to help champion the programme of improvement projects.

Gaining commitment

If the analysis of issues and root causes has been concluded properly, the identify of the few really key projects will be clear. More difficult may be the enlistment of senior management support for a programme of specific projects designed to bring about fundamental change.

The way to do this is to identify a small number of natural champions at a senior level who will sponsor and manage each project. This process can be very revealing as it makes clear which of the senior management team have the willingness and ability to drive the desired changes. As part of the process, the senior management sponsors will be expected to define project terms of reference, assign responsibilities and address critical issues such as budgets and resources. This will reveal whether or not the company has enough committed people, with the right skills and experience to make it happen.

Outline project plans must be prepared by the project teams and general costs identified. Examples of business and project plan templates are shown in Appendices D and E. It will be key to this process to develop a clear understanding of project deliverables and business benefits such as cost reduction, revenue improvement and improved market share. Unless these projects fairly and squarely deliver specific business benefits, they deserve to run into opposition, because *Delighting Customers* should mean improved business performance.

In order to gain full commitment, it will also be important to sell the projects actively to the organization, along with the costs and benefits. Sponsorship by senior executives is key. They must be tagged ahead of time in order to secure their ownership and willingness to support the project before it is even presented as a proposal. A key expense will be the amount of senior management time involved to make this happen. Do not underestimate this cost. A small project office will be needed to support this senior management initiative and to facilitate the work of numerous other players who will make contributions to the *Delighting Customers* programme.

To gain credibility for this analysis, and the projects which result, it is crucial that the project team has been seen to do its homework. A diligent analysis including quantification and calibration of the size and scope of the issues must be included. Customer interviews/customers' data must be captured. Employee comments and views, and the results of workshops must be presented as part of both the analysis and the project plan. A major internal communications programme will be necessary to tell employees what has been decided, how the steps in the *Delighting Customers* programme are to be implemented, and how they will be involved. Making sure that everyone understands their individual role in the scheme of things will help to ensure buy-in from the uncommitted within the organization. Getting the support of the uncommitted majority is a major driver of change. This is discussed fully in Step 8 – making change happen.

Lastly, the best practices of world-class organizations need to be used in support of the case. Best practice is another important driver of change, and its practical value is analysed as part of Step 8 (page 119).

What will the programme look like?

To be successful, the whole programme should be reviewed and approved by the senior management team. Below, we outline what a typical programme looks like.

As an example of a programme of projects, Oracle UK identified a game plan comprising six key projects which taken together are viewed and managed as a single programme of change. We present this programme in Figure 5.7.

In a similar way, Northern Telecom Europe has a strategic plan which focuses the energies of the organization into particular areas designed to improve significantly customer satisfaction (see Figure 5.8). These programmes are the drivers for breaking through the customer satisfaction barriers in their pursuit of more than 95% customer satisfaction.

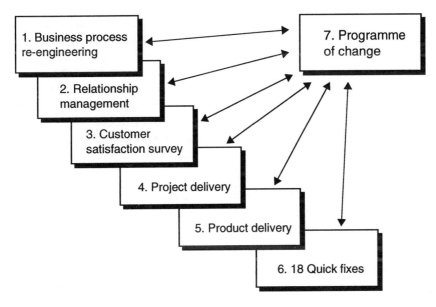

Figure 5.7 Oracle's programme of projects.

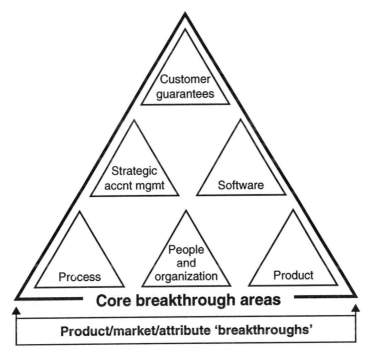

Figure 5.8 Northern Telecom's customer satisfaction strategic plan.

These examples illustrate clearly that to be successful, customer-driven programmes require substantial depth, breadth and commitment. Inevitably, the programme must include on-going measurement of what is important to the customer. They demonstrate the importance of focusing on a small number of projects which strike at the heart of customer issues and drive the vision forward. In each example, the projects are well understood by a critical number of key players within these organizations to ensure that sponsorship is forthcoming.

Conclusion

Now, the senior management team will be committed to an overall game plan which seeks to address the most obvious shortcomings between the service vision and existing business practices. This plan will include:

- a critical mass of named individuals who are committed personally and publicly to each of the projects;
- an understanding of where the most obvious improvements to customer satisfaction are required;
- an assessment of the organization resistors to change within the organization; and
- a number of projects which form the programme of change and focus primarily on the obvious root causes of customer dissatisfaction.

Inevitably, one of the projects will include the establishment or refinement of a permanent process for capturing the voice of the customer (customer feedback system) and driving the programme of continuous change discussed in Steps 4–10.

Having secured commitment for an overall programme, the next step is to outline each project in detail and to undertake a risk assessment so that the organization can make a final go/no go decision.

AT THE END OF THIS STEP . . .

There will be a critical mass of named individuals who are publicly committed to the major projects which form the programme of change.

STEP 3 – THE GO/NO GO DECISION

THE KEY QUESTIONS TO ASK . . .

- What is the overall probability of success?

- What are the risks and benefits associated with each major project?

- Can the organization afford the necessary investment of money and key human resources?

- Does the organization have the will and ability to become customer-driven? If not, stop now!

Having identified an overall game plan, the key strategic and tactical initiatives must be costed and rigorously assessed as projects. This is the mobilization phase of the programme, shown in Figure 5.10, which elaborates on the KPMG DPE model illustrated in Step 2.

This step requires careful project planning, including a risk assessment. The organization must assess the specific risks involved, the ambitiousness of the scope, and the size of the investment required in order to determine the probability of success.

For example, take the case of a relatively small, young and successful company in a growing market. Such an organization can reasonably contemplate major changes, with a view to becoming a world-class service provider in their markets of choice. Consider another example of, say, a nationalized industry in France or the UK. Stagnant markets, adverse political influences and trade union pressure can make change almost impossible. Here, the conclusion may be to focus management effort on changing the rules of the game (e.g. privatization) rather than pursuing a costly initiative to improve customer satisfaction with a limited chance of success.

These examples illustrate the need to be perceptive about the impact of change given the psychological and social dynamics of the organization. The organizational politics must be understood thoroughly in order to make an accurate assessment of risk.

At the end of this step the organizational leaders must make the go/no go decision for each key project.

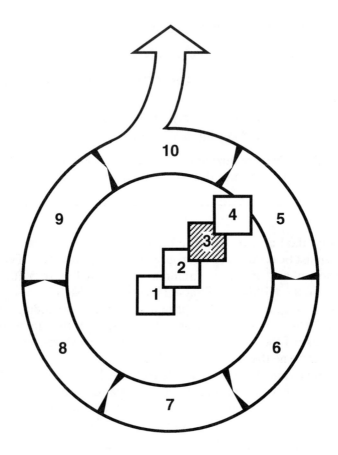

Figure 5.9 Step 3 – the go/no go decision.

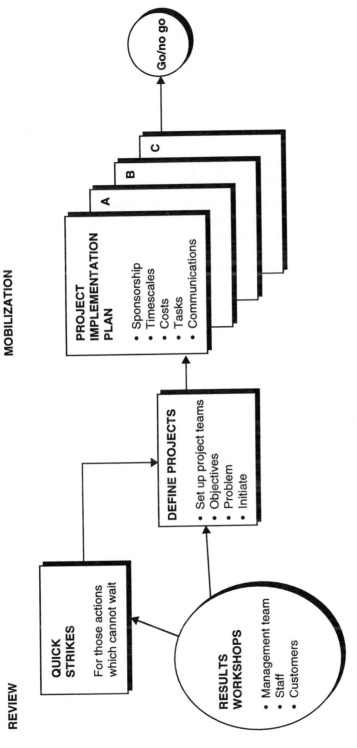

Figure 5.10 KPMG DPE model (continued).

Manage each initiative as a project

Each specific project will need a timetable, an analysis of the business case, and a detail of the resources – all the project disciplines that one would normally include in, say, a large technology project. Project management disciplines are critical. An example of the Oracle UK project plan illustrates the diligence involved and is shown in Appendix E.

As part of this step, a plan needs to be prepared for each specific project and should typically include:

- project definition, goals, objectives and scope:
- named executive sponsor and steering committee members;
- named project manager, probably full-time, and the project team members;
- identification of the commercial, organizational and customer satisfaction risks;
- a budget which includes the total investment required to resolve already-identified issues, and which includes incremental expenses and the number of days of effort to reflect opportunity costs;
- a budget to develop a permanent process for capturing the voice of the customers and driving continuous improvement (see Steps 4–10);
- time scales, review points, and specific phased deliverables; and
- criteria for measuring the impact on the customer, commercial success of the project and specific, tangible business benefits.

This project by project approach is practical and the costs and benefits are easier to assess in this way. In our experience many initiatives, particularly those with a title of Total Quality, have invested a lot in process issues, such as process improvement training. In our view, successful change programmes should focus primarily on those activities with direct business benefits. Unless training delivers a business advantage, it should be a secondary issue. The Trustee Savings Bank, for example, has the right priorities – it concentrates on training staff to solve specific problems and improve processes, in particular those that directly affect customers.

Consider the risks

Risk analysis is vital in order to maximize the business benefits of the programme. In our view, it is possible to select a relatively small number of projects which improve customer satisfaction, where the business benefits are evident, and the probability of success is high. This will be important for two reasons.

1. There is no reason why such projects cannot make contributions directly to the bottom line. Those projects without tangible benefits should be treated with extreme caution.
2. Some early victories will be important for the success of the programme as a whole and for the individuals within the organization who support it. Key individuals will be investing both their time and their personal credibility. Projects with a high risk of failure will not attract the best talent and, if the project does fail, the chances of gaining support in the future from these key people will have been jeopardized.

In order to build further momentum for such changes it will be appropriate to launch some quick win projects which from a risk point of view are 'no brainers'. Pick a few of those well-known issues around the organization that everybody has complained about for years but nobody has got round to fixing. A classic example might be the lack of customer parking or the handling of telephone messages from customers.

Some of the quick-fix opportunities pursued by Oracle UK as part of their customer satisfaction programme are summarized in Appendix E. In this example, each quick-fix project has an executive sponsor and a project manager, and the business case is well defined.

Organization roadblocks are the biggest headache

Managing organizational change is the most difficult roadblock to overcome and requires particular attention. It will be important to assess explicitly the degree of resistance to change. This represents a critical element of project risk. The extent of such resistance needs to be well understood. Examples of resistance may include:

- restrictive business practices such as those embedded in trade union agreements;
- compensation schemes which drive particular styles of behaviour;
- the overall organizational culture, which is difficult to measure; and
- poor internal communications which can also have a major impact on initiatives of this kind.

This analysis of resistance will require an understanding of what sorts of behaviour are required from individuals and teams. List the key individuals in the organization who have the willingness and ability to lead this kind of change and make it a success. Our experience supports the view that attitude is everything. Obviously, those people with the wrong attitude, or the wrong management philosophy, pose the biggest threat and decisive action is called for. It may involve transferring people, or it may necessitate certain people being removed from their jobs. This is not for the faint-hearted. This step requires strong leadership and commitment from the very top – otherwise failure is likely.

The go/no go decision

At this point, the organization should integrate all the project plans so that the value of the individual projects and the merits of the programme as a whole can be considered. A risk assessment should be carried out on each project to determine the likelihood of success. The management team will now be in a position to make the final go/no go decision for each of the individual projects and the programme as a whole. Each go decision will represent a significant commitment and investment of resources. This will include not only financial resources but also a major commitment of time on behalf of the executives and key managers in the organization. Management time can be one of the heaviest costs associated with projects of this kind.

Conclusion

Having made all the go/no go decisions, the organization will have a detailed plan of intervention and an overall programme of change. Specific business projects will have been identified and allocated appropriate resources, business deliverables and time scales. Now, the organization will be able to drive these projects through in a very determined way, having secured the authority to proceed, agreed the necessary sponsorship, obtained approval for the funding, and put the key players and teams in place.

Where customer service is concerned, actions speak louder than words. If projects are judged to be under-resourced or under-funded, do not be afraid to make to make a no go decision. The organization's efforts will be spent better in finding the resources and justifying the costs than in setting off on a path to inevitable failure.

A further cautionary note. As soon as the company proceeds with a customer-driven programme, the expectations of customers and employees will be raised significantly. Failure to deliver real benefits will leave customers disappointed and employees sceptical. Therefore, if the organization is not deadly serious and confident of success, it should STOP NOW!

Should the organization decide to proceed, the next step will involve the establishment of a continuous improvement process based on an accurate understanding of what is important to customers.

AT THE END OF THIS STEP . . .

The business will have in place the key elements that ensure success – a game plan which integrates the key tactical and strategic projects, the organizational commitment and the psychological contracts. If the company is not deadly serious and confident of success, it should STOP NOW!

Chapter 6

Measuring what is important to customers

INTRODUCTION

This next phase will determine the company's success in making the transition to a customer-driven organization. During these steps a permanent process will be set up to capture the voice of the customer and drive through a programme of continuous change.

Much of the work to be undertaken is detailed, time-consuming and laborious. Do not be tempted to cut corners. If customers are not identified and segmented accurately, the organization will end up wide of the mark when it sets its success criteria, and even further adrift from the real world when processes are put in place for measuring customer satisfaction.

STEP 4 – SEGMENTING THE CUSTOMER BASE

THE KEY QUESTIONS TO ASK . . .

- What are the particular needs of specific customers in different markets?

- What is the nature and quality of the business relationships with key customers?

- What role does the organization play in the success of its customers?

That different customers have different needs is a truism. Industry segmentation is valid but other variables area also important, such as the size of the customer organization, their political context and the specific types of service they are receiving. Customers can be segmented in many different ways, including geographically, demographically, behaviourally or by type of relationship.

This provides a backdrop to understanding the relative contribution that the organization makes to the business success of customers. What role does the company play now and where could and should it add most value to its customers? It is equally important to understand the maturity of the relationship. For example, is the firm perceived as a commodity supplier or as a business partner?

Different organizations in different industries may have widely differing requirements in, say, the procurement process. A 'one size fits all' approach is inappropriate. We need to define the service needs of each market and each customer segment. In some cases, a segment may be represented by just one major account customer. The service needs which customers value most may include:

- revenue generating and differentiating products,
- speed of delivery,
- advice during implementation,
- hands-on training, and/or
- the ability to respond fast when things go wrong.

The organization will need to establish which service attributes it should focus on.

Another important area for consideration will be those groups of people who influence the perceptions of customers: the press, professional associations, consultants, market analysts, and others.

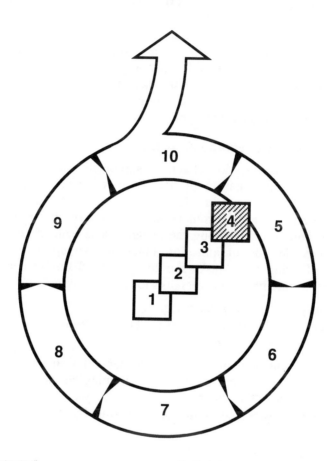

Figure 6.1 Step 4 – segmenting the customer base.

The objective of Step 4 is to segment customers into groupings of needs and expectations, and to verify what is being offered today against what each of these groups wants today and expects tomorrow.

Segmenting customers correctly will take time but it will provide a solid foundation for the efforts which follow. The activity should not be rushed. Marketing teams and business partners will have a valuable contribution to make, and involving them minimizes the effort required, integrates existing segmentation into the *Delighting Customers* programme and extends involvement to more key players.

The customer segmentation process

What follows next is a flow of activities that will guide the organization through the segmentation of its customers. The output from this exercise will also be used in Steps 5–9, in setting the success criteria, gaining feedback from customers, analysing the results, making change happen, and communicating the progress and benefits to customers, employees and those organizations that shape perception.

The following three tasks should be carried out to complete the customer segmentation process, as shown in Figure 6.2.

1. Identify who the customers are.
2. Determine what the customers are being offered.
3. Customer segmentation.

This will create a set of four customer segmentation matrices for every customer, or customer grouping, containing all the segmentation information needed for the *Delighting Customers* programme. The complete set covers (see example in Appendix B):

1. customer / product details,
2. product and service attributes,
3. success criteria / communication activities, and
4. customer (survey) feedback methods.

A customer grouping is one or more customers that share a unique set of needs and expectations in relation to the organization's products and services. Hospitals, global accounts or government offices constitute typical customer groupings. Customer groupings are normally identified by marketing departments as part of their product launch and enhancement programmes. However, it is important to take a fresh look, with their involvement, from the *Delighting Customers* standpoint. In our experience, further groupings will be identified.

The need to segment customers in this way is supported by research carried out by Forum Corporation, whose findings show that this approach can also result in improved customer/supplier relationships.

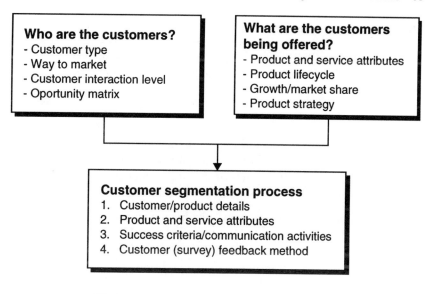

Figure 6.2 Customer segmentation matrix.

BUSINESS EXAMPLE

Forum Corporation, 1993
The customer-driven sales organization

This study began by identifying a broad sample of companies in eight industries in three distinct areas – North America, the United Kingdom, and Hong Kong. Care was taken to ensure a mix of regional, national and multinational companies of different sizes based on number of employees.

Using an open-ended format, 341 in-depth interviews were conducted with buyers responsible for high-level buying decisions, salespeople (selected by customers for their superior performance), and the sales managers of these high-performing salespeople.

Overall, the study concluded that the relationship between customers and sellers is more dynamic and complex than in the past. One of the key findings was that:

A framework that segments customers according to what they need and value can be used by salespeople and sales organizations to create more customer-driven sales approaches and relationships.

Who are the customers?

The customer segmentation matrices to be found in Appendix B can be completed only after the organization has established who its customers are and what they are being offered.

In this first task we look at the customers, which fall into two main groups:

1. those that purchase the company's products and services to use or to sell on (this category will include 'internal' customers for products and services from other parts of the organization); and
2. those that shape the opinions of the purchasers.

The purchasers and users want products and services. The opinion shapers need information – information about the company, products and services and, most importantly, the benefits being generated by the *Delighting Customers* programme. As we will discuss in Step 9, the opinion shapers can be influenced by actively marketing the information in much the same way that the organization markets its products and services. It will require an equal amount of effort. When dealing with a *Delighting Customers* programme, perception is all-important.

Another variable to be considered will be the distribution channel – the way in which the products and services reach the customer. The different relationships between the supplier organization and different types of customer, and opinion shapers, are summarized in Figure 6.3.

Let us now look in detail at the customer types within each group from a perception standpoint.

Purchasers and/or users of the firm's products and services

These are the direct, channel (distributors and dealers) and indirect customers that form a perception of the company's products and services based on their experience with the organization, its products and services.

For each customer type there are three main levels of interaction between customer and supplier organizations:

- the product and/or service level;
- the relationship level (covering more than one product or service); and
- the strategic level (typified by partnerships or joint business planning).

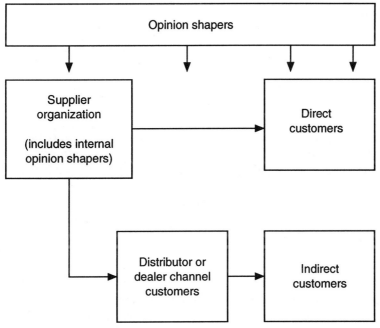

Figure 6.3 Customer types.

Each level demands a different type of customer/supplier relationship, based on differing expectations of the organization's products and services. Customer needs differ significantly between these levels of interaction. Consequently, this breakdown needs to be taken into consideration when customer groupings are being selected.

Companies that invest time and effort in a customer-driven programme are looking for two things – increased customer loyalty and increased business performance. It follows then that a key measure of success will be the satisfaction level of those groups in the customer's organization that represent the purchase decision makers as well as all other personnel that have an influence on the purchase decision makers. This latter group normally includes the influential users of the organization's products and services as well as the senior management team or departmental heads.

Each of these groups has an impact on the purchasing process.

- Users – often initiate buying process, define specifications and influence re-buy decisions.
- Influencers – influence buying decisions and provide information for evaluation purposes.

- Buyers – have formal authority for final selection and are involved in final negotiations.
- Decision makers – have the power to select or approve the final suppliers. This is the customer group that would be selected for the purpose of customer satisfaction surveys.

Opinion shapers

These are the companies, organizations, institutions and individuals that form an opinion of the organization, its products and services based on information gathered . They have an important influence in shaping the perceptions of the customers above.

External opinion shapers include the press, market analysts, consultants, professional associations, the business community and key customers. Internal opinion shapers will include those employees and sales teams within the organization that influence customers and help to shape their perceptions.

The opinion shapers need to be kept updated on the company, products/ services and the benefits that the *Delighting Customers* programme is having on customers. Gaining the interest of these groups in the early stages will require considerable effort in the way of resources and funding. Once the business has develop a reputation in this area, the opinion shapers will start to take the initiative when they want information. In both cases, it is important to target efforts carefully to balance the costs against the benefits gained.

Most companies have personnel or departments that are responsible for external communications and public relations. In these cases it is often just a matter of integrating the customer satisfaction benefits into existing activities. It is important to manage the communications with these groups as they shape both current and future perceptions of customers. This element of the programme is discussed in Step 9, page 129.

The output from this task will be used to set up the customer groupings and complete the customer details shown in the Segmentation Matrices of Appendix B.

What are customers being offered?

To complete this second task we need to determine the following:

- What is the organization offering customers?
- How is this positioned in the product life cycle?
- How well is the business doing?
- What is the product strategy?

To understand what an organization offers its customers requires a detailed look at product and service attributes, product life cycles, growth/market share and product strategies. These are the areas that need to be considered when assessing customer perceptions of products and services. To increase levels of satisfaction, the organization will need to know how its products are positioned in the market, the role that they play in the customer's organization, and the contribution they make to the customer's success. Is the organization a strategic partner, a product (black box) supplier, or both?

This investigation also provides a base of information that will help to determine the appropriate customer feedback methods, success criteria and communications activities in later steps of the *Delighting Customers* programme.

Let us look first at what the organization is offering its customers.

Product and service attributes

Professor Theodore Levitt of the Harvard Business School devised an effective way to think about the customer's needs, with the total product concept diagram which we reproduce in Figure 6.4. (Each dot represents a specific activity or a tangible attribute of a product. Included with the 'expected product' ring, for example, are delivery

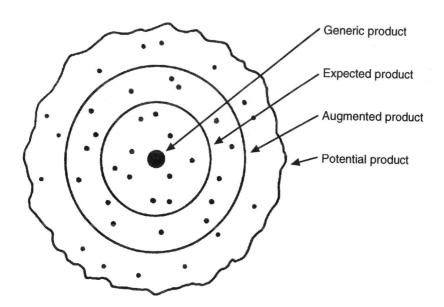

Figure 6.4 The total product concept.

conditions, installation services, after sales services, maintenance, spare parts, training and packaging inconvenience.)

Levitt points out that even if the firm markets a seemingly simple commodity – such as a chemical benzene – the 'product' is much more than that. The 'expected product' customers will buy may need to include such things as the right delivery schedules, payment terms and technical support. The 'augmented product' includes more than the expected product and includes the range of 'extras' that are created to make products and services more attractive and more distinctive – such as application and development support for chemicals, or the industry sector reviews and detailed balance sheet analyses issued to customers by most stockbroking firms. As more businesses offer new augmentations, customers' expectations rise.

The 'potential product' is where the biggest opportunities are for delighting customers. Beyond asking customers what they need, the organization must go further to find the latent needs they may not even be aware of. The potential product offers the opportunity to respond to these newly-identified needs. The attributes identified here should be those that add most value for the customer, and are not simply 'gold plating'. It is important that future needs and expectations are also addressed.

This analysis will identify the full set of product and service attributes to be measured within the *Delighting Customers* programme and the information would be included in the Segmentation Matrix 2 which is included in Appendix B.

We have successfully used Professor Levitt's total product concept to identify our set of attributes. You may choose to use other techniques. Whichever approach is used, we recommend carrying out the first stages of the process in two separate sessions with customers and their employees, before finalizing the areas to be tracked in a joint session. This discussion should centre around customer and employee perceptions of present and future products and services. It should result in agreement on the key attributes and performance measures to be covered in a survey programme.

We also recommend that experienced consultants or reasearch agencies are used to manage this activity. Some are listed in Appendix A. In addition to their expertise, their independence will be invaluable in extracting the best from both groups. Importantly, they will be free from any of the politics that may surround product development or existing customer relationships.

Let us now look at the effects of the product as it moves through the product life cycle.

Product life cycle

The classic product life cycle includes four phases:

- introduction,
- growth,
- maturity/saturation, and
- decline.

As part of understanding what the organization is offering customers, it will be necessary to establish the position of each product in this cycle as it will define the limitations/advantages for *Delighting Customers*.

Let us now consider the profitability and potential of the product within the marketplace.

Growth/market share

All organizations need to establish a balance between well-established cash-generating products or services and those which are cash-consuming. This involves decisions on which products to encourage, develop and maintain and which to phase down and phase out in order to keep a flow of cash running through the organization. This choice will have an impact on the support services that can be delivered. For this reason it will be important to understand where in the portfolio each product is positioned, and to define for each product whether it is:

- a market leader,
- new to market,
- a cash cow, or
- non-profitable.

Lastly, we need to consider the impact of the chosen product strategy.

Product strategy

There are four commonly used product or service strategy options.

- Market penetration – selling more of the same product to more of the same type of customer. This may involve taking market share from competitors or selling more to existing customers.
- Market extension – finding different types of customers or different channels for products.
- Product development – developing new or modified products and services to sell in current markets to existing customers.

- Diversification – combining product development and market extension tactics to sell a new product in a new market.

Every time a product or service is amended to attract new customers, there is the attendant risk that existing customers may be lost as a result of the changes. Against this must be weighed the danger of allowing products and services to become outdated or overtaken by more sophisticated offerings from the competition. An effective way to minimize these risks is to measure continuously what is important to customers.

The strategy that is in place for each product will have an impact on the service offered and on the opportunities for delighting the various customer groupings that have been selected.

The output from the assessments of product and service attributes, life cycle, growth/market share and strategy, will be used to complete the product details in the Segmentation Matrices 1 and 2 as shown in Appendix B.

Customer segmentation

Having assessed who the customers are and what they are offered, it is now a simple exercise of completing Segmentation Matrices 1 and 2 for each of the customer groupings and product lines. Segmentation Matrices 3 and 4 can be prepared for use in Steps 5, 6 and 9 when we consider the success criteria for a *Delighting Customers* programme, customer feedback systems and communications with customers, employees and opinion formers. (Templates for all these matrices are included in Appendix B.)

Conclusion

By undertaking this analysis thoroughly, the organization will obtain a clear view of what it can offer customers, what their needs are, the product's limitations, and the biggest opportunities for *Delighting Customers*. It also highlights many of the gaps between what the organization offers currently and what the customers need and expect.

The prime requirement for *Delighting Customers* is to align the organization's product and service/strategy with customers' needs and expectations, and then to measure and improve performance in each of these areas. The mistake that many companies make is to measure their performance first without checking the alignment of what they offer against what their customers need. Then they wonder why they seem unable to drive up customer satisfaction levels.

In the next step we develop the success criteria for each customer and product segment.

AT THE END OF THIS STEP . . .

Customers will have been segmented according to their needs and expectations, and the organization will have verified what is offered today against what the various customer groupings want.

STEP 5 – DEFINING THE SUCCESS CRITERIA

THE KEY QUESTIONS TO ASK . . .

- How will the organization measure the success of the *Delighting Customers* programme in business terms?

- How will the company measure and reward teams and individuals when operating in its chosen service plane?

In this step we look at identifying and setting the success criteria for the *Delighting Customers* programme, and briefly consider the rewards of success.

A balanced score card is required to assess business success. This can include measures such as:

- repeat business,
- margins,
- market share,
- customer valued metrics,
- the use of each customer as a reference site, and
- customer and employee satisfaction.

These measures can be used to evaluate the performance of individuals, account teams, business units and the company as a whole.

By this stage, the strategy and approach to customer satisfaction have been defined and the service planes and customer segments have been identified.

The objective of this step is to identify the success criteria at the company level, for each business unit and each of the customer groups identified in Step 4. The information can be recorded on the segmentation matrix shown in Appendix B.

Where do the greatest opportunities lie?

The bridge between customers and what the organization offers forms the customer/supplier relationship, which has three levels of interaction – product /service, relationship and strategic.

However, as can be seen in Figure 6.6, there are two other important dimensions to consider:

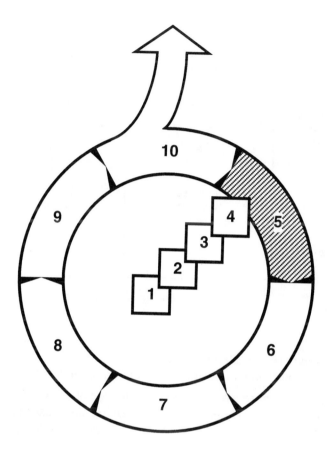

Figure 6.5 Step 5 – defining the success criteria.

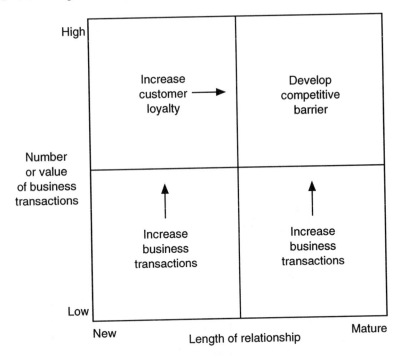

Figure 6.6 Opportunity matrix.

- the length of the relationship, and
- the number/value of business transactions completed.

Using this approach it is possible to establish where the biggest opportunities are. These may lie in driving up satisfaction levels to increase the amount (value) of business transactions, increase customer loyalty and to develop a major barrier to competitor entry. Irrespective of the length of the relationship, if the number (value) of business transactions is low, the success criteria of the firm's *Delighting Customers* programme should be aimed at increasing business. Only when the firm has gained a reasonable number (value) of business transactions can it afford the investment required to develop customer loyalty and a strong barrier to competition.

Maximum impact on customers

Setting the correct success criteria is important, but it is even more critical to kick-off the activities that will drive up customer satisfaction. Customers do not want talk. They want action. The success criteria should be set quickly and involve customers and those employees responsible for meeting the criteria set.

The success criteria should not be complex. They should be easy to understand and be seen as relevant to the direction of the business and needs of the customers. The approach should focus on a small number of key areas that will have the maximum impact on the customer and a high probability of success. The success criteria should demonstrate the company's commitment to customers and the building of a customer-driven organization.

The **ten step approach** is based on continuous improvement. Once the key improvement activities are under way, it will be possible to refine the success criteria in line with the impact that current efforts are having on the customer. This will ensure that all the issues are addressed at the time when the probability of success is highest. Timing is critical in a programme if change.

For each customer grouping identified in Step 4, there should be no more than ten key areas where success will be measured. Typically, there could be three measures each at the customer (account) level and the product/market business unit level, and four at the company level.

The success criteria set at the company level will be common across all customer segments. The success criteria at the business unit and customer levels will vary according to the product being offered and the needs of the customer.

The key to making this work will be to task every level with improving a few critical areas. Any more than three or four is unmanageable. Business must continue and not everything can be fixed straight away. Once three or four issues have been resolved, the organization will have sent a clear message to customers and employees that a serious commitment has been made. When it comes to eliminating the next three to four issues , there will an increased likelihood of buy-in and support from both customers and employees.

Let us now consider the process for setting the specific success criteria that the organization will adopt.

Setting the success criteria

Start at the company level by noting (or re-confirming) the overall success criteria for the *Delighting Customers* programme. (These will have been established during Steps 1–3, dealing with vision and service planes.)

With these criteria in mind, review the customer and product details for each of the customer groupings established in Step 4 to identify the success criteria for the corresponding account (customer) teams and individuals/departments involved in providing the products and services to that customer group.

Based on this information the key success criteria can be set for each business units (by product and/or region) and associated functional groups/departments.

The criteria set at the company level now need to be revisited again to make sure that they underpin the success criteria that have been set for the business units. If necessary, the company level success criteria should be added to or modified.

This top-down then bottom-up approach to setting the success criteria ensures that both business and customer needs are met. All the success criteria should be developed with the involvement of customers, the senior management team, account teams, business unit heads and employee representatives. Each set should be signed off by those responsible for meeting the success criteria.

With this information available, the customer segmentation matrix established in Step 4 (see Appendix B) can be completed. This will provide the organization with a credible document for use in setting employees' and managers' objectives, bonuses, etc. In our experience, people focus on the areas for which they are rewarded. If they are not being rewarded for meeting the success criteria that have been set for them, the rate of progress will be limited.

Northern Telecom's customer satisfaction programme provides an example of the success criteria set at the company, business unit, department and account level. (The customer, country and product names have been removed.)

BUSINESS EXAMPLE

Northern Telecom

COMPANY LEVEL – SUCCESS CRITERIA

To deliver market leadership through customer satisfaction, superior value and product excellence, Northern Telecom has set the following success criteria for its near-term objectives:

- A customer satisfaction level of 95%
  (This is measured by a global customer satisfaction programme carried out by independent research agencies.)
- Employee satisfaction of 95%
  (This is measured by a global annual employee survey programme.)
- 12% global industry market share
  (Northern Telecom uses outside industry sources to calculate

its worldwide share of the product and service markets in which it competes.)

- 15% minimum rate of return on equity
  (This figure is calculated by dividing net income by the total shareholders' equity. This is a measure of the financial health of the business.)

BUSINESS UNIT – SUCCESS CRITERIA

Example 1 – consistent and thorough communication with distribution channels

- Integrate customer events
  (a) European Distributor Alliance Council
  (b) product seminar
  (c) marketing forum.
- Streamline contacts – all functions.
- Increase the number of face-to-face meetings.

Example 2 – full integration and communication of the enhanced new product introduction (NPI) process

- Involve distribution channels.
- Formalize information flow.
- Control frequency and forecast of NPI.

Example 3 – to migrate account teams

- Move from a pure 'technology sell' to that of a 'solutions provider' organization.
- Do this by means of clear account planning and targeting of key account decision makers.

DEPARTMENT LEVEL – SUCCESS CRITERIA

Example 1 – product delivery

- Improve delivery and quoted lead times from the current eight to twelve weeks to (ultimately) four weeks.
- Initiate a process to make available 'off the shelf' products.

Example 2 – sales and marketing

- Re-focus the sales team to sell applications and services, to meet customers business needs.
- With an understanding of the customers needs, develop product plans to ensure that the right product is available to the market at the right time and at the right price.

Example 3 – personnel

- Provide effective customer care training.
- Develop on a regional basis, training programmes that will increase the level of understanding of the local business needs.

ACCOUNT LEVEL – SUCCESS CRITERIA

Example 1

Establish links between Northern Telecom Research Group and Customer X's Research Group on joint development projects focusing on the three- to five-year time frame.

Example 2

Introduce more clearly-focused project marketing teams in Northern Telecom, to address all aspects (technical through to marketing) of Customer X's requirements in the business services marketplace. The teams must effectively mirror Customer X's market focus, in order to make Northern Telecom easy to do business with for Customer X's emerging global business.

Example 3

Country X to have more direct local control over the research and development allocation to product development. Customer X will increasingly demand differentiating features and service offerings as their competition grows. Competitor X is strong because of their focus and responsiveness to Customer X's needs. Product A's software evolution offers an opportunity here at the new application layer – the same needs to apply for integrated access solutions.

The success criteria above are a small sample of the many hundreds of initiatives within Northern Telecom. Every level focuses on three to four areas and these are co-ordinated to ensure that they are supportive of each other.

To measure the effectiveness of Northern Telecom's success criteria, customer satisfaction targets are set each year at the account, department, business unit and company levels. This ensures that the initiatives are focused on driving up satisfaction in a way that can be reflected by their customers in the independent customer survey programme. Below this level, customer satisfaction objectives are set for all employees to focus the improvement activities and to involve the individual in meeting the targets that are set.

Conclusion

The key to the success in this step is to task every level within the organization with improving a few critical areas that will have maximum impact on the customer and take the business closer to being customer-driven.

In our experience, linking performance in *Delighting Customers* with compensation schemes is key. It would be nice to be able to say that people naturally focus on the customer at the cost of everything else. The truth is that in the complexities of business today, most managers and employees have more to do than they have time for. When the pressure is on, the majority of people concentrate their priorities most closely on the areas for which they are compensated. *Delighting Customers* can be an easy area to wriggle out of unless suitable measures and rewards are in place.

If there is no objective to increase customer satisfaction, and no clear link between customer satisfaction performance and compensation, then the change programme will be at the mercy of time and an individual's conscience. For such a strategic programme this is too high a risk to take. It only takes one person in the chain to upset the customer to undo the work of many others.

Setting out clear objectives and rewarding performance will provide a level of control that makes it easier to manage a customer-driven programme effectively.

As we shall see in Step 6, capturing the customer viewpoint provides both a major driver of change and the clearest assessment of progress towards meeting the success criteria for the *Delighting Customers* programme.

AT THE END OF THIS STEP . . .

The success criteria will have been defined for each customer grouping and at every level throughout the business.

STEP 6 – CUSTOMER FEEDBACK SYSTEMS

THE KEY QUESTIONS TO ASK . . .

- How can the organization capture the customer's viewpoint most effectively?

- How will the business quantify what is important to customers?

- How important are confidentiality and independence in this process?

A comprehensive customer satisfaction survey programme is essential as a method for listening to customers and as a measurement of progress. The quality of the feedback mechanism will have major impact on the credibility of the *Delighting Customers* programme and the results should rapidly become a key driver of change and a rich source of continuous improvement opportunities.

The objective of this step is to establish the feedback methods for each customer group and the related success criteria identified in Steps 4 and 5. Following this step the organization will be able to complete Segmentation Matrix 4, the customer (survey) feedback, in Appendix B. This will record the selected feedback method for each customer grouping.

Quite simply, the key success factor for this step is to ask the right questions and capture what is most important to the customer.

Preparing the organization

As a starting point, the organization must prepare itself by asking two questions.

- What are the specific objectives of the survey for the company as a whole and for each of its customer groupings?
- What are the main priorities?

Without the answers to these questions, there is a real risk that the survey will result in a mass of information that the organization has not prepared itself to deal with.

Wherever an organization decides to focus its attention, it is important that the feedback enables performance to be assessed against

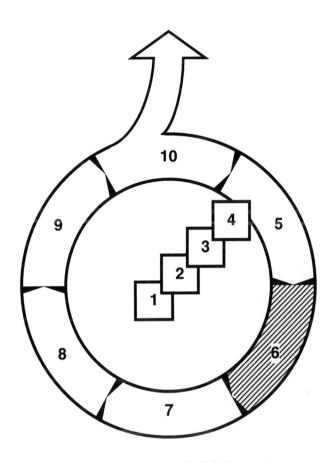

Figure 6.7 Step 6 – customer feedback systems.

the service vision that was established in Step 1 (page 46) and the success criteria set out in Step 5 (page 90). The questions asked should reflect what is important to the customer not what is important to the supplier. Ultimately, the success of a customer survey programme should be judged against the changes that are made as a direct result. Closing the loop is vital – as illustrated in the virtuous circle shown in Figure 6.8 and documented further in Step 8 (page 119).

The importance of closing the loop is demonstrated by the example of a high technology company which recently spent a significant amount of money on a customer survey. The analysis was conducted by an independent consulting company with good credentials. The result was a professional and comprehensive summary of how customers viewed the company, its products and its services.

There was only one problem. Having received the report, the organization did not know what to do with it. As a result nothing happened.

This kind of trap can be avoided by working with the senior management team to determine their particular issues, objectives and

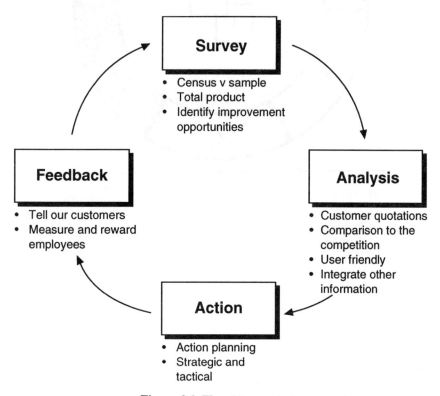

Figure 6.8 The virtuous circle.

priorities for customer feedback data. To be effective, this will require a dialogue with most or all of the team. 'Hot buttons' for senior managers might include how a particular target market views the organization with respect to a particular competitor. Another area of interest might be the customer view on the problems associated with a particular product or service. Quantifying the exact nature and size of a problem from a customer's point of view can set the agenda for putting things right.

It is important to establish the precise requirements of senior managers because these will provide a target against which to orientate the survey and position results in a way that helps to sell change. The guiding rule, however, is to focus on what is most important to the customer.

Designing the survey process

At the outset, the company will need to consider the kind of feedback it requires and the most practical means of obtaining it. A number of issues must be considered:

- Is it highly quantitative or qualitative?
- What methods will be used to collect the information?
- How acceptable would a mail-out questionnaire be for the managing director of your largest customer?
- Who will be the target audience for communicating the results?
- How will the results be presented?
- How will customer satisfaction levels be calibrated?

It is essential to acknowledge that the customer's perception is reality. This can lead to some interesting debates with the engineering and statistically minded individuals in the organization!

In our experience, when designing a customer survey programme, the essential aim should be to reveal to the organization the key headlines, not a mass of statistically elegant detail. These results will lead to further detailed analysis.

The detailed design of the customer satisfaction survey programme is by no means a simple task. It will involve many trade-offs between competing requirements, starting with the definition of who the customers are. As discussed in Step 4, there will be different types of customer, from major international accounts to the smaller business. Within each account, there will be different kinds of individuals, from senior executives at or near board level to junior people who may use the product or service.

Consequently, in Figure 6.9, we have included a useful checklist to help with the design of the survey process.

There are some fundamental elements which will be reflected in the objectives of a customer satisfaction survey programme. At the very least a customer survey must identify the few key dissatisfiers that currently characterize the relationship with customers. This will be important as the first improvement step will be to focus the activities and the energies of the organization on removing dissatisfiers. In the light of the first survey, the organization will have a first agenda item – to compensate for past misdeeds and remove those obstacles which aggravate customers.

Moving from a reactive response to a more pro-active approach, a second requirement will be to look at the future needs of customers and

---

A checklist for designing the survey process

1. **What are the objectives of the programme?**

2. **Approach**
   - census or sample
   - media: postal questionnaire, telephone interview, face-to-face meeting, user group, focus group?
   - will it identify performance ratings?
   - will it capture re-purchasing loyalty?
   - will it capture competitive performance?
   - will it capture existing, potential and lost customers?
   - will it identify improvement opportunities?
   - will it capture verbatim comments?
   - is local language a key issue?
   - pilot the survey?

3. **Target audience**
   - partnership (executive)
   - relationship (account) and/or
   - product/services (buyers/users)

4. **Questionnaire**
   - align with target audience (CEO? Buyers? Users?)
   - expected response rate
   - structure
   - length: time, number of questions
   - product focus and/or service focus?
   - relationship and/or strategic focus?
   - calibration of views: rating scales?
   - frequency of tracking?
   - event driven?

Figure 6.9 A useful checklist.

identify specific opportunities to improve and evolve existing products and services. Geoffrey Woodling of the Business Futures Network emphasizes this point:

> It has been said that many organizations will have to learn how to adapt to future challenges. Learning will undoubtedly be a very important characteristic of organizational behaviour. But it must be more than learning to perfect the past, making current methods and practices work better to satisfy past expectations. There are clearly no shortages of information in many organizations about their customers. What is lacking is any understanding of their customers' future expectations.

Checklist continued

5. **Feedback of results**
    -   target audience
    -   format: user-friendly, innovative
    -   comparison to competition
    -   ranked importance
    -   trend analysis: database structure
    -   integrate other data e.g. results of employee satisfaction surveys, marketing surveys, company image survey
    -   consultant reports

6. **Closing the loop**
    -   customer and employee involvement
    -   response management: tactical and strategic action plans
    -   data analysis tools
    -   how will results/action plans be tied to compensation?
    -   customer, employee and business communications
    -   how will results drive new product/service developments?
    -   how will results drive 3-, 5-, 10-year business plans?

7. **Project team**
    -   sponsor, project manager ...?
    -   industry experience of independent consultants/interviewers?
    -   is confidentiality an issue?
    -   business unit co-ordinators
    -   customer account representation
    -   supporting tools, databases

Figure 6.9 A useful checklist *(continued)*.

The survey method must be designed to address the need for information of this kind. Face-to-face interviews, focus groups, customer workshops and feedback sessions are all useful for this purpose.

The third requirement for the survey will be to influence fundamental change within the organization. Using independent data in a quantifiable way about what customers are saying will help individuals to lead the organization and to influence change.

A very simple way of gaining employees' attention and making them change their behaviour is to use actual customer quotations that will grab their imagination. A striking example came when customers were asked to compare one organization against another by personifying the two companies. They characterized the principal competitor as tall dark and handsome and the client organization as short, fat and boring. Reactions like this can have a dramatic impact on the executive management team. Such simple quotations can invoke significant emotional response and subsequently drive rapid action.

In another real life example, the executive management team of an international blue chip company was astonished and embarrassed with some of the comments made by individuals of a major account customer. Comments such as 'We don't trust those b------' certainly gained the attention of the board.

Let us look in more detail at questionnaire design, because it holds one of the keys to the quality of the information that will be collected.

Questionnaire design

There are numerous variables that can influence the structure of the survey questionnaire:

- Will it concentrate on particular products or services?
- Will the questionnaire target particular major accounts?
- Will the data be viewed geographically by sales region or vertically by market sector?
- What do the customers in the financial services market, for example, think of your company as compared to those in the manufacturing sector?

Many organizations deliver their products and services using different channels, and this can provide another view against which to design the questionnaire and the structure of the overall survey programme.

Appendix C includes some examples of questionnaires and survey designs. Completion of the segmentation matrices covered in Step 4 (page 78) and Appendix B will also assist the choice of an appropriate survey method for each customer grouping.

Typically, a questionnaire will be designed to address some of the following areas:

- overall levels of satisfaction by vertical market, by major account customer or by product line;
- levels of satisfaction for operational functions such as marketing, personnel installation, support and training;
- detailed and specific feedback on the attributes of particular products, and relative importance of features such as ease of use, cost, reliability and functionality;
- an understanding of the quality of the business relationship with key accounts;
- customers' rating of the organization against certain competitors.
- repurchasing loyalty;
- perceived capability of meeting future needs;
- specific opportunities to improve products and services; and
- ideas that customers have to offer.

Questionnaire design is also influenced by the way it is to be administered. The choice includes a mailed questionnaire, telephone and face-to-face interviews or a combination of these approaches. It is important to decide how long a customer will be prepared to spend answering the survey questions. Anything beyond 20–25 minutes is too much time to expect a senior manager to devote to answering a questionnaire.

A questionnaire must also measure each customer's response to the basic question: 'What is your overall level of satisfaction?' This is of particular value because it provides a punchy headline. As a piece of data, it can be used across products, across vertical programmes, vertical industries, vertical markets and as a measurement over time. Such simple headline statistics offer an easily grasped measurement of progress and a useful benchmark against the competition.

The questionnaire must also assess and reflect the key attributes of the products or service at hand. Levitt's total product concept is useful in this respect because it encourages a view of a total product that comprises a range of elements such as price, speed of delivery, warranty, training and support. It also looks at current and future needs and those special attributes that add most value to the customer.

As an example, ICL use some 37 measures to assess the total product, including a full range of product, service, relationship and quality issues (see Figure 6.10). ICL also uses customer and internal focus groups to obtain valuable feedback from clients in what it calls a 'real time perceptions survey', summarised in the brief example below.

The 37 measures used by ICL

1. **Product characteristics and performance**
   - Measure up to their original specifications
   - Perform reliably and well in use
   - Can be upgraded and improved
   - Meet business needs in terms of features and price

2. **Range and quality of services**
   - Availability of consultancy, design and implementation services
   - Right skills and knowledge to help your business
   - Relevant and accessible range of training courses
   - Trainers have right knowledge/presentation skills

3. **Corporate image and reputation**
   - Well established and respected in the market place
   - High calibre and effective managers
   - Committed to quality in manufacture, services and support

4. **Meeting promises and commitments**
   - Meets promised delivery dates
   - Makes honest and realistic claims about products
   - Gives clear commitments to your company
   - Staff keep their personal promises and commitments

5. **Responsiveness and professionalism of staff**
   - Communicate clearly, honestly and appropriately
   - Deal quickly and effectively with problems/enquiries
   - Provide clear and effective points of contact
   - Communicate well within their own organisation

6. **Quality of customer service support**
   - Prompt and efficient handling of service calls
   - Staff listen carefully and are helpful and dependable
   - Staff know products and provide technical advice
   - Service staff fix equipment correctly and quickly
   - Staff available and effective at sorting out problems

7. **Quality of sales interface**
   - Show honesty and integrity in their dealings
   - Quick and reliable access to technical information
   - Take responsibility for sorting out problems
   - Can be reached easily when necessary
   - Build up long-term relationships with customers
   - Timely and relevant information on product changes
   - Enthusiastic about winning and keeping business

8. **Easy company to do business with**
   - Provide clear and accurate invoices
   - Documentation is relevant and easy to use
   - Put you in touch with right people when you call
   - Understand business/needs in quotations/proposals
   - Show flexibility in its terms and conditions
   - Keep you regularly informed about progress

Figure 6.10 The 37 measures used by ICL.

BUSINESS EXAMPLE

ICL

In ICL's own words;

> Surveys are a good method to gather numerical feedback from clients on the total service we provide but they are limited in the amount of anecdotal feedback to tell ICL what they really feel. In addition surveys usually are sent to only one person, at most a small number of people, on the client site.

As a result, ICL has developed an additional process which aims to:

- involve more client staff;
- gather feedback from them on their perception of ICL;
- involve all the ICL people who work with the client;
- work systematically on developing a plan to change the service offered;
- improve the perception of ICL; and
- share the plan with the client.

Twenty questions were developed; they are based on the five key service qualities established by long-term research in the USA, namely: tangibles (products plus service), reliability, responsiveness, assurance and empathy. At a real time event, client staff vote individually on the importance of each of the twenty questions and the performance they see from ICL. Voting is displayed on a grid and the facilitator draws out from the client staff where there are differences of opinion or where ICL operates in a 'danger zone'. This provides the starting point for gathering the client perception of ICL's opportunities for improvement.

As the next stage, a more detailed event is run for those ICL staff (from sales, customer service and technology divisions) involved with the client. The staff vote on the same twenty questions and comparisons are made between the staff and client views on the importance of issues and on ICL performance. This highlights two new danger zones – where issues were important to the client but not to the staff; where the client viewed performance low but staff rated it high. The ICL staff then look at the results of the client perceptions and danger zones. These three assessments are then used as the basis for discussions on opportunities for improvement. According to ICL:

> The end result was a prioritized improvement plan which could be driven by the account team and shared with the client.

Before we conclude this section, there are a few other factors which are worth mentioning that will influence the effectiveness of the survey process.

Other pointers

First, as we established in Step 4, it is important to define the different kinds of customer within a specific business account. Such definitions typically include decision makers, influencers, experts and users. When measuring what is important to customers in large, complex organizations such definitions are mandatory.

It follows that it is inadvisable to use a single questionnaire design to capture all points of view. It may be equally unwise to consider using the same survey medium for all customers in the sample. For example, a mailed questionnaire to an accounting supervisor or a software programmer would be entirely appropriate. They may be quite happy to spend time completing a lengthy questionnaire. Such an approach is likely to be less popular with a senior executive in the client organization, whose views would be better sought by conducting a personal interview over the telephone or, preferably, face-to-face. This is a more expensive option, but the results are more reliable and of a higher quality.

Having defined who the customers are, the accuracy of contact data needs to be checked thoroughly. The name, address, mailing address, postal code, telephone number, etc. for each chosen respondent must be verified. There are no short cuts to building a database of detailed information. To set up such a programme requires working closely with members of the account and marketing team. It requires a lot of hard work, but the benefits gained from the survey will reflect the due diligence and attention to detail paid in this step of the survey programme.

Second, account team members will need to spend a significant amount of time on the laborious detail of assembling and checking contact information. To encourage them, it will be necessary to demonstrate that there is something in it for them. In our experience account teams respond well when they appreciate that they will be getting valuable account intelligence. Make sure they know that the detailed comments and feedback will be made available to them and that they will be involved in every step of the programme. There may be a tendency for some sales divisions to pick tame accounts who will, mostly, make favourable comments. This can be avoided by using strict selection criteria, such as the size of account by revenue.

The next point to make is that the frequency of a survey programme can be varied. In our view, major account customers should be surveyed annually. The drip-feeding of results also works well. Rather than surveying all customers at one point in time, the surveys can be staggered over four quarters. This has a double advantage. It spreads the workload and the voice of the customer is heard continuously through the year.

Finally, there is the matter of the survey timing. Event-driven surveys can be useful. For example, three months after a major sale or installation of a particular product or service, the 'system' may generate a questionnaire. Advantage can also be taken of conferences and other opportunities where a large number of customers gather together as events for capturing customer comments. Regular trending surveys will be required for the company and its defined customer groupings to monitor progress against the targets set.

In our view, surveys should be undertaken professionally and independently to ensure that they are both effective and credible. The choice of independent consultants will be crucial. In our experience, there are numerous well-qualified experienced consultants in the market. Customer satisfaction surveys are a mature discipline. We strongly recommend using those independents who specialize in your industry. A list of research agencies is included in Appendix A, together with details of the controlling research associations that cover Europe and the United States.

In conclusion, once customers have been asked for their views and comments their expectations will have been raised. Asking them what they have disliked in the past, and what needs to be improved in the future, will set the expectation that things are about to change. It is crucial to understand that unless the organization is prepared to take this information and translate it into change, the business runs the risk of actually driving down customer satisfaction. The simple rule is not to ask questions that the business is not prepared to respond to!

Now, the organization will have matched customer feedback methods to each of the customer segments and associated success criteria. Target groups should have been identified for follow up and improvement activities. The next step that we need to consider is how the results should be analysed, how to make change happen and how to ensure that improvements are communicated successfully both internally and externally.

> ### AT THE END OF THIS STEP . . .
>
> A customer feedback system will have been designed for each customer grouping throughout the business.

Chapter 7

Delighting customers

INTRODUCTION

With the right customer feedback system in place, the business will have a regular health check on its progress towards its customer satisfaction goals. Now the organization needs to invest in interpreting the data and converting it into actionable information.

As the programme develops, the broad-brush view of customer needs and expectations becomes focused increasingly on the specific requirements of individual customers or the shortcoming of particular products and services. This puts the spotlight on the *Delighting Customers* team and the processes it has designed to make change happen.

Delighted customers are the prime objective of the entire programme. An orgianzation must aim at having customers who will queue to obtain that organization's services, who will make the first move and who will want to set up partnerships. Such customers will consciously promote the company's products and services to others, and they may even happily pay a premium!

STEP 7 – ANALYSING RESULTS

THE KEY QUESTIONS TO ASK . . .

- How will the results of customer feedback be interpreted and help to build a customer-driven organization?

- Who will analyse the results?

- Who will be responsible for service improvement and evolution?

The people who best understand the customer and the market place should be given the responsibility and authority for interpretation of the results and planning and delivering an organizational response. Ultimately, results must drive change. Otherwise the whole exercise is futile. In driving such change, it is vital to establish priorities against business objectives and decide on the best approach to take. Identify a manageable number of quick-fix opportunities as well as those that require longer-term solutions at a root-cause or systemic level.

The objective of this step is to develop a process to analyse the results and to produce action plans that drive tactical and strategic improvements. These activities will form part of a continuous organizational learning process. Data analysis tools should also be developed/purchased to ease the analysis of the data and to identify the target improvement areas that will have the most impact on driving up satisfaction levels. Organizations can choose between analysing the data themselves or using the experience of research agencies or consultancies.

There are three fundamental elements which drive success during this step of the customer-driven programme.

1. The results must be credible. They must be quantifiable, mathematically correct and methodologically sound. They must be brutally honest. For total integrity, the survey must be conducted by an independent research organization (details of these organizations are included in Appendix A). Failure to get this right can lead to arguments between executives about the validity of results. It offers individuals excuses to hide behind and provides a justification for doing nothing.

2. The results must be action-orientated. They should be contained in

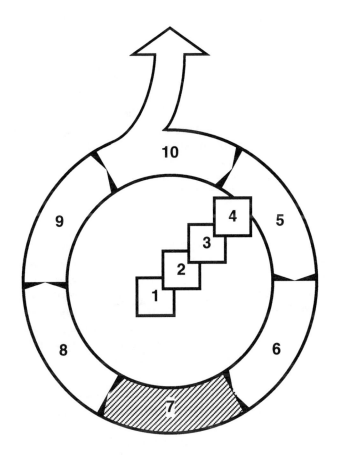

Figure 7.1 Step 7 – analysing results.

the form of a recommendation report and action plan, and they should make changes and improvements compelling, inevitable and unavoidable. The inclusion of verbatim quotations from major account customers can inspire – or sometimes embarrass – the organization into taking urgent action.

3. The results must have operational implications. They must be part of a formal process which drives action planning and operational outcomes in order to close the business loop. Such action plans should drive change at two levels. There must be improvement initiatives at a structural level, directed at fundamental business procedures, and quick-fix initiatives at the tactical level which can be undertaken by local improvement teams.

Let us now discuss these three elements in more detail.

Credibility of results

Because people trust the results provided by independent third parties, they can be used as an effective means of influencing people to change their behaviour. Professional independents will be well versed in the art and science of conducting customer satisfaction surveys and have the necessary investment in the infrastructure required to support comprehensive surveys. This would include, for example, statisticians, computer-aided telephone interview facilities, relevant industry experience, and knowledgeable interviewers who can speak local languages as required.

The numbers of customers interviewed must go beyond the thresholds required for belief. For the survey to be successful, the data must be statistically valid and comprehensive. It cannot be purely anecdotal. In addition to the quantitative data, the results should also capture qualitative information. This can take the form of verbatim quotations, which add flavour and a human touch, and answers to open-ended questions. The independents must not be encouraged to sanitize the comments which may be unpalatable to the organization. There is no point in asking customers what they think if nobody is going to listen to what they say.

Getting attention

In order to get across the key messages it is important to be able to communicate the results effectively and in a way that invokes a 'hearts and minds' response. The information needs to be digested easily by busy people running a business. There are numerous standard ways of presenting such material and these include, for example, importance versus performances, and comparisons with the competition.

The first example in Figure 7.2 shows measures of customer satisfaction for various product and service attributes. These results are compared to the relative performance of the organization's strongest competitor. Analysis of the size of variance is useful, as it enables an organization to identify competitive strengths and weaknesses as a basis for setting the priorities for subsequent courses of action.

The second example, Figure 7.3, presents a graph of customer satisfaction for attributes against their relative importance to customers. Here, attribute B falls into the category of high importance/low performance and clearly presents a priority for improvement. Further examples are given in Appendic F.

The independent research organization should provide an overall report which carries the key headline messages for people to digest. To ensure that the results are taken seriously, it may be necessary for the recommendations and conclusions to go to the board. In this event, the use of a blue-chip international consultancy will usually carry the most weight.

The results should be broken down in accordance with the market segments and customer groupings we defined in Step 4. This will give more detailed feedback, for example, at a major account level or by vertical market, to help executives and sales teams to extract maximum value from the information. Additionally, an overall score of customer satisfaction will serve as the benchmark against which to compare future results.

In summary, the results of the survey must be compelling in order to drive action. As a direct result, the question on everybody's lips should be:

What are we going to do now?

and the immediate response must be:

We must do something.

Doing nothing must not be seen as an option at this point. If people can even consider doing nothing, the survey has not done its job and this step in the *Delighting Customers* programme has failed.

Operational outcomes

The final report summarizing the results of the customer satisfaction survey must include recommendations for next steps in order to close

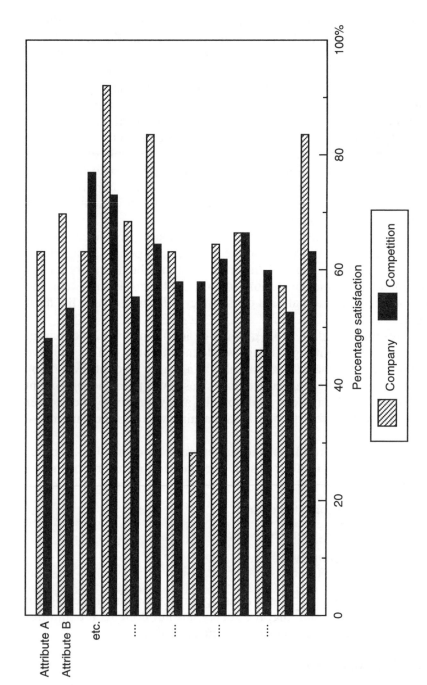

Figure 7.2 Performance against strongest competitor.

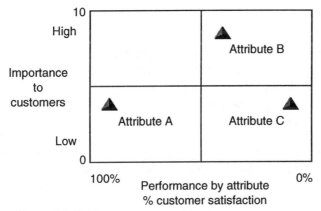

Figure 7.3 Performance versus importance to customer.

the loop. That is, detailed action planning and a related process must be an integral part of this step. Specific priorities and quick-fix initiatives must be identified. A small number of priority issues can be assigned to individuals along with deadlines by which to prepare action plans for follow up.

Typically, action plans will be at two levels:

1. There will be those customer issues whose root causes centre on the system itself. They reflect the fundamental nature of the organization as a system and may impact existing business policies. These issues are properly addressed by the senior management team because they may require changes to business processes or policy, a new strategy or a significant investment.
2. There will be continuous improvements to be made by people at the sharp end. These are the sort of projects that can be undertaken by local improvement teams.

The survey may generate numerous customer issues, not all of which can be tackled simultaneously. It will be vital to focus on a small number that will have the most impact on customer delight.

Avoid the trap of treating the symptoms rather than root causes. Let us say, for example, that customers complain about documentation for certain products. The simple solution is to make sure, via local action, that the customer receives the appropriate documentation. The root cause, however, may be in the product group and shipping group who delivered the manuals in the first place. Unsurprisingly, the customer survey the next year reveals the same customer still complaining about the same problem. Thus, beware of fixing only symptoms without addressing root causes. Clearly, both must be addressed.

Conclusion

By now, the organization will have developed a process to analyse the results of the satisfaction survey and produced action plans to drive the tactical and strategic improvements of greatest importance to customers. It will be important to manage this as an ongoing programme of organizational change. It should be seen as a continuous learning process and a specific means of becoming a customer-driven organization.

The survey results will have been analysed and a view taken on the response required. In addition, organizations will have identified the other key projects which form the overall programme of change. Next we consider the successful route to making change happen.

AT THE END OF THIS STEP . . .

There will be a process for analysing results and producing action plans to drive tactical improvement and structural change.

STEP 8 – MAKING CHANGE HAPPEN

THE KEY QUESTIONS TO ASK . . .

- How will the organization be made to change in response to customer feedback?

- How will continuous service improvement be driven through a combination of quick fixes and long-term organization re-engineering?

A detailed understanding of the sources of customer dissatisfaction and identification of improvement opportunities are essential starting points for this next step. The primary concern now should be a planned set of focused initiatives and some engineered quick wins. The development of these activities must have the involvement of those people who best understand the customer, who have the authority to change policy and who are responsible for implementing the improvements.

During this step the organization will develop a change management programme to facilitate the successful introduction of the improvements identified by the customer-driven programme.

The changes should be designed to delight customers, to exceed their expectations. Just satisfying customers will not be good enough. Satisfied customers may still go elsewhere if they get the right offer such as a cheaper price. Delighted customers will think long and hard before risking the unknown of another supplier. They will be looking at the task that they face in satisfying their own customers. To have a supplier that is customer driven and to exceed their expectations is a significant business advantage and not one to give up for short-term gains.

Delighting Customers is an obvious business strategy and one that most companies find easy to accept. However, when faced with implementation it suddenly becomes a daunting task that many see as an unattainable goal. This is a natural conclusion given the depth of changes that most companies need to make. It may be painful but it is achievable. We have witnessed a number of companies that have turned their organizations around and are now perceived as being truly customer-driven. British Airways and Rank Xerox are prime examples.

- How does the company tackle a task that for many organizations appears insurmountable?
- How can it delight customers?
- How does it become truly customer-driven?

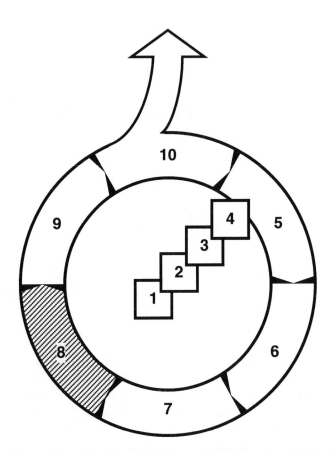

Figure 7.4 Step 8 – making change happen.

In our experience this is best achieved in three consecutive waves:

1. eliminate the major dissatisfiers,
2. satisfy a high percentage of customers,

but aim to go on to

3. delight a high percentage of customers.

With this gradual approach the challenge becomes more manageable. As each stage is reached, the benefits will be felt and the organization will have a solid platform together with the organizational skills to undertake the next phase. This is about organizations in the world of *Delighting Customers*.

When organizations first start out they are faced with the barrage of new skills to learn. The task seems daunting. But as you develop your organizational skills, a self-understanding develops with an awareness of strengths and weaknesses. As organizations mature further there will a new confidence in approach, pulling on experiences and on the network of friends and associates that have been made along the way.

As a business embarks on this journey, one thing is for sure. Change will need to take place in every nook and cranny and at every level of the organization.

In the following sections we outline a structure for change and discuss some of the key drivers to make change happen.

Structure for change

The model shown in Figure 7.5 is a structure for change, and one that we have found to be successful. It facilitates the integration of knowledge and efforts, and has three levels of change:

- account level (customer interface),
- business unit level (including departmental or functional level), and
- company level (strategic and company-wide initiatives).

The purpose of this structure is to provide a clear link between the customer and the strategic management of the company. The number of levels can be increased or reduced, depending on the structure of the organization and its business practices. Change will need to be managed at every level with a method for escalating common issues and addressing areas that are not making progress.

Change at each level is driven by continuous improvement using an interconnected virtuous circle approach which starts with inputs from the customer or a customer change review meeting. This data is then

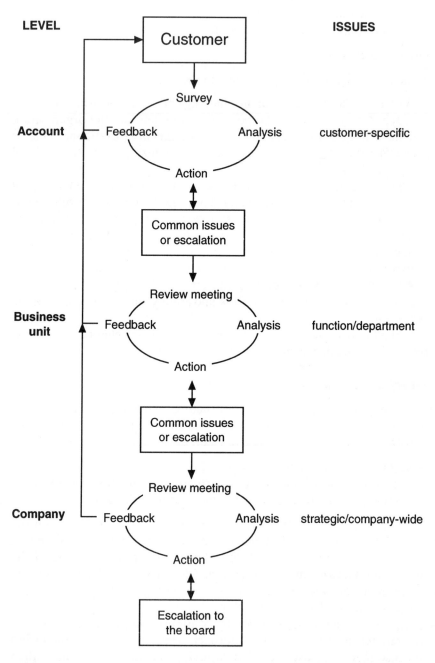

Figure 7.5 Making change happen through interconnected virtuous circles.

analysed and appropriate actions are put in place. Progress is regularly monitored and the feedback is provided to the customers and employees throughout the process. The process then starts over again with the next input from the customer or scheduled review meeting.

Each level would have its own programme of improvements and success criteria. Actions would typically have a mix of quick wins and medium- to long-term improvements. The bulk of these would be addressed within 6 to 12 months. A communications plan would exist for customers, employees and other influential areas, both internal and external. Each change loop would have a named person accountable for implementation and the achievement of agreed success criteria.

The improvement and communication plans are consolidated into a co-ordinated programme at the company level. This structure turns the *Delighting Customers* programme into a manageable change programme to support the journey to becoming a customer-driven organization. It also provides a platform for the organization's leaders at every level to demonstrate their commitment by driving through improvement initiatives vigorously. In Appendices D and E we give examples of business and project plan templates to help manage the change programme.

The Northern Telecom Europe business example discussed in Step 5, page 94, illustrates the types of improvement initiatives that would typically be in place at the different levels within an organization and how together they form a co-ordinated programme to make change happen.

Drivers of change

In implementing *Delighting Customers* programmes, we have also observed a number of activities – or drivers – that facilitate or speed up the change process. Leadership and culture are among the most obvious and most powerful drivers of change, and these have been discussed in Chapter 2. Compensation, or individual financial reward has been mentioned as another driver and was discussed in Step 5 in the context of success criteria. We have also observed other activities that have made a dramatic impact on the change process. They are:

- the use of best practice,
- motivating the uncommitted majority,
- accountability, and
- employee empowerment.

The use of best practice

The value of best practice has been raised already during Step 2, as a valuable means of persuading the organization's leaders of the value of *Delighting Customers* programmes. It can have an equally profound effect as a driver of change at every level within an organization from company-wide to customer processes and practices.

Once an area for improvement has been identified, it is normal to assemble a team to resolve the issue. Many solutions will be available to the team. Often a new process will need to be developed, such as a reward and recognition scheme. linked to delighting customers. This raises vital questions. Which solution should be chosen? For new processes, should the team start from scratch? At worst, the team may end up trusting the new changes to trial and error.

When new problems are encountered, or where the team lacks the expertise to understand fully the solutions available, change becomes a high risk area. People and organizations offer only one chance to get things right. If the solution does not address the problem, the sceptics are seen to be proved right and the organization may be reluctant to support any future changes in this area.

In all cases, but especially in the areas of high risk, the use of best practice safeguards the way forward. Some effort will be required up front to research possible best practices, but the time spent will be recouped by the confidence in approach that can be taken during the implementation phase. If a process represents best practice, it will have a high probability of success and will provide the proof needed to win over the sceptics.

There is no need to re-invent the wheel. Best practice can come from within the organization or outside. Take the example mentioned above of putting in place a customer satisfaction reward and recognition scheme. A similar scheme may already be in place within the company to reward quality achievements or technological innovation. Studying the process at first hand and talking to the users and process owners will provide an understanding of the methodology used, its shortcomings and its benefits. If a suitable practice is not available internally, look outside to other companies and organizations.

An understanding of the principles of benchmarking is essential, but more important is the development of a network of like-minded companies that are willing to exchange their best practices. Most quality-related organizations support benchmarking and the sharing of best practice between their members. Joining these groups is a way of developing a personal network, almost overnight. Among the most important organizations in the field are:

- the European Foundation for Quality Management,
- the British Quality Foundation,
- International Benchmarking Clearinghouse,
- The Benchmarking Centre (UK),
- The Strategic Planning Institute (USA), and
- the Swedish Institute for Quality.

Business associations, user groups, customers and suppliers may also prove a fertile source of best practice activities. The methodology and approach used to research and implement best practice is important but it is more important to keep focused on the need to find the solution to problem areas under review. Benchmarking is a means to an end. Do not get bogged down with the detail. It is full of jargon and surrounded by expensive consultants. Talk to others that have found best practice. They will be very willing to share their experiences and the approaches they have taken.

For example, Northern Telecom Europe carried out four best practice studies to develop and sustain their customer-driven programme. This gave them the confidence in approach and thoroughness of back-up to get them through the early barriers to change and win over disbelievers. By successfully marketing the data and selling change, it kept *Delighting Customers* as the number one item on the president's agenda.

By being able to learn from these studies the company now has in place a customer satisfaction strategic plan and an implementation model that are driving them towards being a truly customer-driven organization. As a result of the best practice studies, the company has been able to develop a mature programme for customer satisfaction in half the time taken by some of the companies it benchmarked. Best practice implementation and people involvement have been the keys to their progress and this formula is now working in other areas such as employee satisfaction.

Motivating the uncommitted majority

There is a saying that:

> Those that sit in the shade won't take an axe to the tree.

The same can be said for the uncommitted majority.

Customer feedback systems will capture the bad news and it is only natural to fight off the need to change. But before these types of programmes can be integrated fully into the culture of an organization, the uncommitted must be motivated.

The fact is that people do whatever they are evaluated on and rewarded for. The 'cause' may be enough to get 'champions' involved, but the sceptics only move when they see their bosses evaluating their performance on the basis of action – in this case *Delighting Customers*.

It will take time to work out how to get them hooked. It may be as simple as getting their boss to ask them to do it. Others may need to be convinced gradually, maybe with a pilot programme. Some may need the big stick. In almost all cases, it will be necessary to be persistent and to sell the reasons for change constantly. The process of marketing successes to build up converts is dealt with in Step 9.

Once the uncommitted have been hooked (aware, interested and motivated), the organization needs to find ways to get them involved, and to make them accountable for improvements. To sustain their support, they need to be rewarded for any successes that stem from their changed behaviour.

Many of the leaders in this field link customer satisfaction improvements to management bonus schemes, sales compensation plans and employee objectives. Recognition, in the form of awards, is also given for the most improved product line and regional area.

The inclusion of customer satisfaction as an element of an organization's salary and compensation schemes is a clear demonstration to employees that improvements in customer satisfaction levels are a frequent expectation of normal business life. They soon come to the conclusion that to survive in the company they need to learn how to delight customers.

Accountability

If it is not possible to put a name to an improvement activity it will not happen. It is too easy for people to ignore activities for which they are not held accountable.

As soon as someone becomes accountable, the problem starts to disappear. Often, improvement activities will cross functional boundaries within the business and a degree of re-organization may be necessary before someone becomes responsible for an improvement initiative. Do not compromise. Insist on someone being held accountable before putting organizational effort into improvement activities. It will pay dividends in the long run.

Trustees Savings Bank, for example, has teams involved in re-engineering its key customer-facing processes and each process is 'owned' by a senior manager who has the authority to implement the necessary changes.

Employee empowerment

Empowerment is a much over-used phrase, but we have struggled to find a an alternative phrase that explains our point adequately.

What we mean by empowerment in this context is giving the people at the closest point to the customer the amount of decision-making power they need to have the flexibility and speed of action necessary to delight their customers. As we stand today, this is opposite to the way most companies are organized. Some are on the journey to an empowered workforce but most have a long way to go. Many organizations have not yet started. A programme designed to delight customers will highlight the need for the downward movement of decision-making powers and for weaving this new style into the culture of the company.

In our experience, empowered workforces are brought about through the setting of a clear vision and an investment in training. The benefits to be gained are immense when it comes to breaking down the barriers to change, although they may not be seen at an organizational level until there is a critical mass of empowered people. For this reason, there may be value in concentrating the available training resources and funds into one area of the business at a time. In this way, the programme can be finely tuned to suit the company culture. The benefits will be easier to see by comparing these employees and customer groups with others within the organization.

The overall objective is to move the existing culture to one of becoming more empowered and empowering. In other words, it should try to provide a personal development opportunity for employees so that they can both create and participate in the change process. The aim should be to give employees the will, confidence and additional skills to be able to act to improve things for the better in their organization and their lives.

Everyone can make a difference – an improvement – through having the authority to exercise choice and action. But the way the programme is positioned can be critical to its success. Within Northern Telecom Europe, it has been positioned as a development task to liberate the potential of individuals. The programme was explicitly not a remedial programme and sought to avoid being seen as a place to be sent in order to 'be empowered'. The training is organized on a voluntary basis and typically reaches 60% of the people in a business unit within 18 months. It is delivered partly by line staff and continues by popular demand.

Delighting Customers and an empowered workforce go hand in hand. This is a long-term driver for change and it may take some managers and employees several years before they are empowered. Others may never make the transition. The way forward is to take full advantage of the areas of the business that have become empowered and use these groups and skill sets to spur on the drive to becoming customer-driven.

AT THE END OF THIS STEP . . .

The organization will have developed a continuous change process to respond to the needs and expectations of customers.

STEP 9 – COMMUNICATING THE CHANGES

THE KEY QUESTIONS TO ASK . . .

- How will the organization communicate back to customers what they have told the researchers and how the business is responding?

- What will be the impact of this response on customers, employees and business partners?

- How will the loop be closed?

- How will the company decide when is the right time to communicate?

In Step 8, we looked at how to make change happen and very briefly at the need to communicate and promote the benefits of change. In fact, effective communications has been a recurring theme throughout the *Delighting Customers* process. It is essential if maximum benefit is to be extracted from the hard work necessary to achieve significant increases in the level of customer satisfaction.

At each stage of the programme, it will be necessary to consider carefully with whom the organization needs to communicate, what the messages will be, and how these messages will be managed and communicated. The management of the communications process is key and requires careful planning. In Appendix G we provide a **communication plan template** to support this activity.

With a *Delighting Customers* programme firmly in place and a feedback system in operation, customer expectations have been raised. Customers will be aware of some of the things that are happening because they have been directly involved. Now, the business needs to be sure that they have a clear view of the total picture as it affects them. In the same way, all staff must be provided with an clear understanding of what is being achieved, how they have contributed and what is expected of them in the future.

However, it is important to ensure that the organization does not over-promise and under-deliver. What is communicated is a strategic decision that needs very careful consideration. It is advisable to wait until there are some measurable improvement in results on which to report. A comparison with the performance of leading competitors may

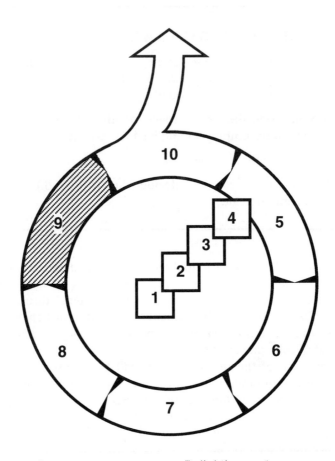

Figure 7.6 Step 9 – communicating the changes.

be important, but telling customers of the progress that the organization has made could rebound if it draws attention to the fact that the business still lags behind others in the market.

The communications strategy will need to be supported by a comprehensive programme which details the objectives, methods, responsibilities and budget. It is preferable to allocate a separate budget to ensure that the communications funds for *Delighting Customers* are not re-assigned to a new product launch or a sponsorship opportunity!

Within Northern Telecom Europe, for example, the communications programme in support of the *Delighting Customers* programme has a separate objective for each of its three primary audiences:

1. **customers** – to show how the company's customer satisfaction process gives it an important competitive advantage and offers benefits to customers that will increase the success of their business;
2. **employees** – to enhance employee understanding of the strategic advantage of customer satisfaction and increase commitment to its successful ongoing implementation; and
3. **business community/opinion formers** – to use Northern Telecom Europe's commitment to the customer satisfaction process as a key element in building the company's reputation as a business leader.

The team approach

The corporate affairs, public relations and marketing professionals within the business should be involved in the development of the communications programme because:

- communications in support of the customer-driven programme should be integrated with the other corporate and marketing messages from the organization; and
- the group responsible for managing the *Delighting Customers* programme cannot afford to operate in isolation.

Specific activities may need to be implemented to meet the particular requirements of major account customers, or market segments that were identified in Step 4. In that case, marketing and public relations people will have valuable input to the account team's planning of a suitable response for communicating the changes that are taking place.

Over time, further objectives will emerge as the *Delighting Customers* programme gains in maturity or as a direct response to new customer and employees needs. Like other steps in the **ten step approach**, communications should be treated as dynamic and subject both to continuous review and to continuous improvement.

The segmentation matrix developed in Step 4 (page 78) and included in Appendix B can be used to develop and record the communication activities for each customer grouping.

Communicating with customers

Here, the account teams – and others at the sharp end of dealing with customers – have the key role to play in communications. But they will need support. Individual customers will clearly have their own views on how they want to receive feedback on the organization's progress towards its overall goals and resolution of their particular issues.

With major accounts, the process is likely to be quite formalized with structured meetings that have a set agenda for review and which are minuted. There may be reports on individual improvement initiatives, particularly where these involve joint action teams drawn from both the supplier organization and the customer. Typically, formal meetings like these would be held quarterly.

Beyond these reviews at a senior level, account team members will be reporting regularly to their customer peers. Credibility with the customer demands that there is a process in place that ensures that everyone has up-to-date and accurate information on the progress of the *Delighting Customers* programme. This will be of particular significance where customer dealings cross a number of divisions, locations and possibly countries. The information may be maintained securely on a central database which gives different levels of access to people throughout the organization.

The actual process of communication with the customer will almost certainly be co-ordinated and managed by the account team itself. It is equally important to communicate progress widely within the customer organization. It may be necessary to set up and maintain contact with all the people that purchase or use the organization's products. As a minimum, there should be regular communication with every customer representative involved in the survey programme.

Similarly, communicating change to customers that do not fall into the major account bracket can be a complex exercise. They will have communicated their concerns via the change loop identified in Step 8 and will be looking for proof that their voice is being heard and that their particular issues are being addressed.

A customer with justifiable dissatisfaction over the quality of product support documentation, for instance, will want specific information on what is being done and when resolution can be expected. However, if there are many thousands – or even hundreds of thousands – of customers, with a similar problem, the level of the response escalates.

They all need to be told what is being done to put things right and it is important that they know – by letter, through advertising, in editorial or in the customer newspaper – before their frustrations are reflected in their next purchasing decision. When the communications envisaged are on this scale, the contribution of marketing, advertising and public relations professionals will be of major importance in both planning and execution.

Direct information from the sales contact will always be the preferred means of communication and that requires that all members of the sales and support team are kept abreast of the *Delighting Customers* improvements as they affect each customer and market segment. They should also be supported with information on improvement activities at the product and company level. The use of information systems, databases and on-line access is an effective way of making this information available to large numbers of people in the shortest possible time.

BUSINESS EXAMPLE

IBM

IBM Havant fully recognizes the value of interaction between customers and employees and runs annual 'customer weeks' where the site is opened up for customer visits. There are displays, seminars, demonstrations, round-table meetings and management sessions to which internal and external customers are invited. All the events are tailored to the needs of customer segments.

Customer weeks have proved very successful in promoting relationships and giving all employees visibility of, and discussion with, customers. In excess of 95% of visitors confirmed that they were delighted with their visit.

Communicating with employees

Throughout the **ten step approach** we have underlined the importance of winning the hearts and minds of the 'internal customers', motivating them and turning their enthusiasm to advantage. We have stressed that most people actually want to provide outstanding customer service. The challenge for management, as we have seen, is to remove the obstacles and invest in new practices that support people in this desire.

Employee motivation is an art in itself and almost certainly it is used extensively by the sales and HR professionals within the organization. Their involvement in the development of an integrated programme in support of *Delighting Customers* will add real value to the programme.

The information needs of different people within the organization will vary significantly. All should be fully aware of the headline news, such as changes in overall levels of satisfaction and the areas of both outstanding and disappointing performance.

Within diverse organizations, dissemination of results at the local level is essential, and there will be opportunities to use existing channels of communication to advantage. People want to know how they are performing against their targets, how that compares with the overall performance of the business and how that, in turn, stacks up against the performance of principal competitors.

Do not underestimate the value of word of mouth within the organization. Work towards *customer delight* being included automatically on the agenda for internal meetings at every level from senior management to departmental briefings and reviews.

With all the broad scale communications, there should be a strong emphasis on striking (not necessarily glossy or costly) visuals. The use of pie charts, rather than text alone, to demonstrate key survey results at local poster sites or in the customer newspaper can be particularly effective.

With the programme for *Delighting Customers* being treated as a 'product' in its own right, the organization can draw on all the proven tools of promotion to build and project a strong brand identity. Consider the use of a creative logo as a focus for the programme, and use the device on all information and promotion material – from report covers to posters for internal notice boards, for the overheads and slides used at customer review meetings, and for sweaters, T-shirts, pens and other give-aways.

Particularly in the early stages of *Delighting Customers*, a small but permanent exhibition at carefully chosen sites can be used to promote the latest survey results and news of other significant developments. The employee newspaper or magazine will be a continuing means of communication, perhaps with a regular section devoted to news and features.

Communicating with opinion formers

When it comes to targeting communications and promotional activities at opinion formers, the segmentations and groupings defined earlier can be used. They should include some or all of the following groups that are shaping the opinions of the customers that purchase and/or use the company's products and services.

Media

They should accurately reflect the organization's competitive positioning in the way they report on the company, products/services and market focus. They should be kept informed on selected customer-driven initiatives, the overall progress being made, and the benefits that have accrued.

Consultants and market analysts

They should understand the customer-driven strategy and support it in their own contacts with the media and other influential groups, including potential customers.

Professional bodies/industry bodies

These groups should be aware of the *Delighting Customers* programme in the context of the organization's wider corporate objectives. They should be in a position to portray the company as a reference source and an expert/ counsellor/innovator in the areas of customer/supplier relationships.

Complementary businesses

Complementary companies serving the same customer markets should be seen to support the organization's approach and convey to both existing and potential customers the benefits that the *Delighting Customers* programme delivers.

Key customers

These may be involved as references and be participating actively in testimonial marketing.

The leadership role

Earlier, in Chapter 2, we dealt at some length with the critical role of leadership in the process. Inspirational leaders cannot operate in a vacuum and without a regular platform. They need outlets – opportunities to communicate the organization's vision and shape perceptions among customers, employees, opinion forgers and the business community at large.

Some opportunities will arise naturally such as the annual report, sales conferences, articles in the organization's own newspapers and magazines, and visits to operating units away from head office. Other outlets – such as interviews with the national or business press, seminar and conference presentations – may need to be created.

Below we have outlined just some of the methods of communication and promotion that can be used to support and reinforce the *Delighting Customers* message with target groups. In Appendix G, we have included a template for the development of a *Delighting Customers* communication plan.

- **Media relations**

  - Inclusion of *Delighting Customers* details in all media information packs.
  - Interviews on *Delighting Customers* in the business context (competitive advantage) with business media, industry sector press and major regional papers.
  - Articles on the programme in business and sector press.
  - News and feature material on the success of specific initiatives – perhaps as joint case studies with customers.
  - Exposure of customer-driven successes at grass roots level for local papers.

- **Literature**

  - Inclusion of the *Delighting Customers* messages as part of all corporate, sales and product/service literature.
  - Preparation of a brochure dealing specifically with the programme.
  - A *Delighting Customers* annual report summarizing the programme, the results, the successes and the aims and priorities for the following year – separate versions could be prepared to meet the different needs of different target audiences.

- **Video**

  - Specific video on the programme for external audiences for it is unlikely that the same video would be equally suitable for communicating with employees.
  - Specially targeted videos for communicating with key account customers, where purchasers and users are geographically dispersed.

● **Customer presentations**

  – Talks and presentations to a customer's own management and staff at their sales and technical meetings.
  – Exhibitions at customer sites.
  – Focus groups with key customers.

● **Seminars and exhibitions**

  – Papers and talks on *Delighting Customers*, given by the organization's leaders at industry-wide and sector conferences and seminars.
  – Production of a 'bank' of overheads and slides in a common style and dealing with all aspects of the programme will simplify the preparation of material.
  – Inclusion of the *Delighting Customers* programme on displays at industry and product exhibitions.
  – A *Delighting Customers* forum for selected customers and industry experts to develop the customer/supplier chain and add real value to the ultimate user.

Conclusion

Closing the loop by communicating change effectively ensures that the organization's focus begins and ends with the customer. It puts all the efforts of the *Delighting Customers* programme into sharp perspective and prepares the way for a possible step change in the service vision.

AT THE END OF THIS STEP . . .

A process will be in place for communicating to customers, employees, opinion formers and other key groups what the organization has learned, what it is doing as a result and the expected benefits for customers.

Chapter 8

Quo Vadis?

INTRODUCTION

Do not underestimate the achievement of reaching this final step in the *Delighting Customers* programme. To reach here the organization will have invested an immense amount of time and effort. Throughout the business, and at all levels, the benefits of culture change and the impact of inspirational leadership will be clear. Equally, the organization will have experienced both the pain and the pleasure that we hinted at in the preface.

Above all, customers will have become more closely integrated with the business. Their voice is being heard and their views are being acted upon. Relationships are stronger.

Now there are new opportunities to be faced and more decisions to be made.

STEP 10 – CHOOSING WHERE NEXT TO COMPETE

THE KEY QUESTIONS TO ASK . . .

- How can the total product be embellished in order to move qualitatively into the next dimension of service?

- What new investment in skills and infrastructure is required for success in this next, higher service plane?

OR

- Will the business choose to remain on the same service plane?

- If so, where will efforts be focused to enhance existing services and effect process efficiencies?

At this stage, the organization is in a position to assess the successes of the programme to date and the firm's willingness and capability to undertake further changes. This review procedure should occur at least once a year and be integrated with the organization's planning and budgetary process to ensure proper and timely funding of any new initiatives that may arise.

Following this assessment, the decision can be taken on where next to focus the organization's efforts. It can move to Step 5 and continue the improvement cycle by re-focusing on service improvements and gaining from process efficiencies. Or, it can step up to the next service plane to gain market competitiveness (see Figure 8.2).

Operating at the higher level service plane will require new metrics, new organizational capabilities, new service delivery systems, more time and almost certainly, additional investment. Steps 1 to 10 will need to be repeated. The same guidelines apply. The difference lies in the fact that the organization will be offering a higher set of service benefits to customers.

The objective of this step is to decide whether or not to move to this next higher service plane. The timing of this step-change will be driven by the organization's vision and strategic goals, as identified in Step 1, or forced upon the company by competition and the pressures of the market place.

This is just another staging post on the journey towards being a

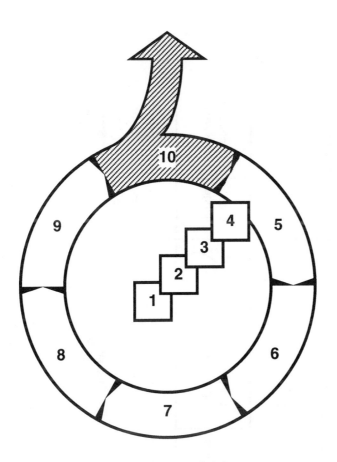

Figure 8.1 Step 10 – choosing where next to compete.

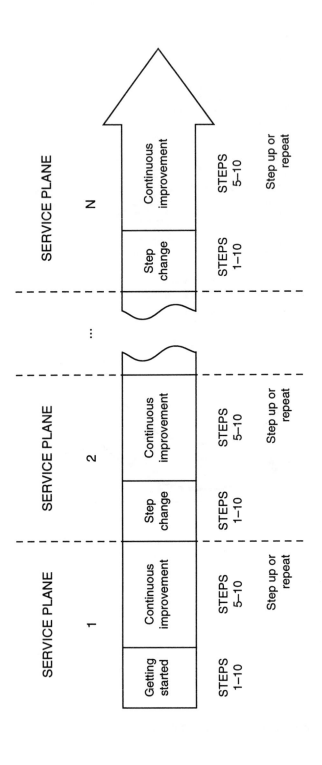

Figure 8.2 Roadmap to *Delighting Customers*.

customer-driven organization. But if all the other steps have been carried out successfully, the step change to the next service plane is the next logical development. In this way, the company can move through the service planes and become a truly customer-driven organization with the ability to delight customers continuously.

Like any business challenge, major change carries its dangers. But the prize for moving the organization up another gear, for *Delighting Customers* at the next service plane, opens up new opportunities for business advantage.

The greatest prize lies at the end of the journey – customer recognition that you have become a world-class performer and strategic business partner.

AT THE END OF THIS STEP . . .

The decision will have been taken whether or not to move into the next higher dimension of service offerings.

Section Three

The conclusions

Chapter 9

How to be a winner

THE KEY MESSAGES . . .

- Increasing customer satisfaction improves sales and profits.

- A balanced scorecard of measures is required to chart progress.

- To effect change in today's business environment requires a structured approach.

- Fix the dissatisfiers first.

- The attitude of an organization is a key predictor of success or failure

- Effective communication with customers, employees and opinion formers is essential to close the loop.

- Inspiring leadership is mandatory for success.

- Involve customers at every opportunity and keep them informed of progress.

- Personalize the programme. Demand that individuals demonstrate their commitment by delivering results.

- Build a multi-disciplinary team.

- Customer-driven organizations have a fifth P in their marketing mix.

INTRODUCTION

As organizations contemplate customer service strategies, it is clear that none of the constraints are conceptual. All the concerns that need to be resolved are human and organizational. In order to become customer driven and world class, there are a number of challenges which organizations must address.

The entire process requires the structured approach set out in the **ten step approach**, which will take the organization through the key steps of assessment, programme planning, implementation and closing the loop. The culture and attitude of the business will provide a simple – and early – predictor of success or failure. A culture that embraces change, experiment and learning has in-built potential for success.

In our opinion, the key messages summarized at the start of this chapter hold the secret to becoming a winner. Some are of critical importance.

THE PHENOMENAL EFFECT OF LEADERSHIP

Inspiring leadership is mandatory for success. It is the key differentiator between those organizations, business units, departments and account teams that have driven up customer satisfaction levels and those that have not.

When faced with issues such as poor market fit, lack of support or product problems it becomes impossible to satisfy, let alone delight, customers. Excuses like these are offered by those who are not leading. We find it interesting that many organizations readily accept these excuses. But this is not always the case.

Even when faced with these insurmountable problems, we have noted that some groups have made significant increases in customer satisfaction levels. The critical difference has been the presence of a strong and inspirational leader who believed in a *Delighting Customers* programme as a major business driver and who made the time to lead.

INVOLVE CUSTOMERS AT EVERY STAGE

Although fixing the key causes of dissatisfaction is important, *Delighting Customers* does not mean being wrapped up solely with today's problems. It is about moving forward, addressing one issue at a time, making progress and demonstrating commitment to customers. Customers know what the problems are. They want the issues to be acknowledged and to see that the organization is fixing them. They want to feel the impact of these improvements on their own business. Above all, they want to be involved.

Involving customers at every stage of the programme will pay handsome dividends as one of the essential driving forces for change and progress within the organization.

PERSONALIZE THE PROGRAMME

Programmes of this kind, however grandly positioned in the hearts and minds of the key players, need ownership by each and every individual concerned. Bring plans down to the individual level as quickly as possible. We have found that personal 'touchstones' help to manifest many of the key initiatives in progress. It is vital to get individuals to sign up, willingly or otherwise, to two or three tasks which are emblematic of their commitment. For example, it might mean a manager agreeing to sponsor project budgets through the business planning process, a business unit manager agreeing to implement new customer satisfaction metrics, or an individual sales professional managing customer expectations by avoiding the temptation to over-promise.

In the early days of the programme, in particular, such touchstones act as a personal litmus test. It is a simple way to determine those individuals, at every level of the organization, who can be relied upon to make change happen.

BUILD A MULTI-DISCIPLINARY TEAM

For strategic initiatives of this kind to succeed a broad range of skills and experience must be mobilized and should include business strategy, marketing, organizational development, human resource management, information systems and total quality management disciplines. In short, only seasoned managers need apply!

Success will result from creating a team of experienced, shrewd practitioners, wily in the ways of getting things done. When it comes to *Delighting Customers* programmes, old and wise will always beat young and keen.

World-class performance results from getting a lot of things right. Success will come from involving those people who know how to achieve results in today's imperfect organization whilst also having the vision and skills to build for the future.

THE FIFTH 'P'

What differentiates customer-driven organizations from the rest? The answer is the fifth P.

The future environment for business is fraught with change. There are very few constants and organizations have little direct control over the variables involved. However, the customer is a constant that will always exist and the products and services that the organization offers offer are among the manageable variables over which it has direct control.

These controlling variables of products and services are generally known as the marketing mix, or the four Ps:

- product (what you offer)
- price (what you charge)
- promotion (what you communicate)
- place (how and where you deliver).

Within each of these areas are a number of options and strategies that can be chosen, and these are mixed to create a set of product and service offerings that will meet the specific needs and expectations of the different types of customers that the business serves.

Customer-driven organizations manage an additional P in their marketing mix – the **fifth P: perception** (the experience that you offer). This perception is gained by customers having experienced the organization's products and services. This can be any event or sum of events from order and delivery through to operational use and support, and it is also impacted by the perception of previous events and the opinions of other influential bodies.

Before customers experience the organization's products and services their perceptions can be positive, neutral or negative. As they experience the product and services this perception will either remain the same or change (see Figure 9.1).

Customer-driven organizations understand this process and research customers' experiences and modify their policies, procedures, products and services by 'designing in' the elements of the fifth P. For example, a

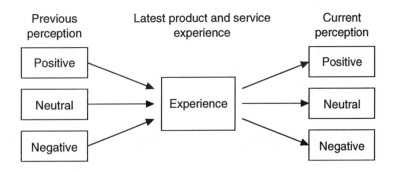

Figure 9.1 Customer perceptions.

key account that purchases a range of products and services from the organization may have a sound relationship with each product group, but their overall experiences of the business could be negative due to a perceived failure to co-ordinate services. Having researched these experiences, the organization can respond by developing a process to improve co-ordination and, in doing so, turn a negative perception to a positive one.

In a complex business-to-business environment errors may occur. When things go wrong customer-driven organizations have the controls in place to protect 'the experience' of their customers. They have determined the procedures and events that will change a customer with a negative perception to a positive perception. In doing so they have gained full recovery from a potentially damaging situation and sustained customer loyalty.

Integrating the fifth P into the organization gives a marketing mix to create a truly pro-active customer-driven organization and a business edge which is the envy of competitors.

CONCLUSION

Experience clearly shows that success results from a combination of hard service engineering approaches and softer people practices.

The implementation of a *Delighting Customers* programme should be managed tightly with all the rigour that would be applied to a large systems or engineering project. Such disciplines would also include methods, procedures, systems and training. This approach should extend to all areas of company operations. In recruitment, for instance, establish the characteristics and experience required to excel in service encounters. Subsequently, the appropriate psychometric tests or assessment centre techniques would be used to ensure compliance.

On the other hand, there is still a place for some passion. As we have seen, inspirational leadership has an important role to play. Customers and employees alike respond positively when they understand a company's ideals – its values and the service proposition. Active communication of these ideals is vital.

In conclusion, delighting customers is all about effective implementation and people involvement. The simple yet profound truth is that *Delighting Customers* is, for most people, a natural and satisfying experience; and a compelling if not mandatory business strategy.

If it is that obvious, why do so many organizations continue to get it wrong?

Appendices

Appendix A

Customer satisfaction research agencies and research associations

Before embarking on the development of a customer feedback programme, we advise you to seek the advice of those organizations that carry out this work for a living – the research agencies. We include a list of the agencies and their controlling association for Europe, North America and Japan. This list is by no means exhaustive but it will enable you to get started. Before selecting a research agency, we advise you to obtain recommendations from the research associations or through your contacts within the business community.

SOME CUSTOMER SATISFACTION RESEARCH AGENCIES

Belgium	Sobemap Marketing SA 5 Place du Champs de Mars Boîte 32 1050 Bruxelles	Tel. 02/508 52 11 Fax. 02/514 32 94
Denmark	Vilstrup Research AS Rosenvoengets Alle 25 DK 2100 Copenhagen	Tel. 354 366 33 Fax. 354 368 16
Finland	Marketing Radar Tietajantle 14 02130 Espoo	Tel. 0/455 45 11 Fax. 0/48 36 28

France	Louis Harris France	
	17 Rue de Louvre	Tel. 1/44 82 25 25
	75001 Paris	Fax. 1/42 53 91 16
	Sofres	
	16 Rue Barbes	Tel. 1/40 92 40 92
	92129 Montrouge Cedex	Fax. 1/42 53 91 16
Germany	Emnid Institut GmbH & Co	
	Bodelschwinghstrasse 23–25	Tel. 0521 28001–0
	4800 Bielefeld 1	Fax. 0521 28001–55
	GfK Marktforschung GmbH & Co	
	Nordwestring 101	Tel. 0911/395–1
	8500 Nürnberg	Fax. 0911/395–209
Greece	Global Link International	
	Marketing Research	
	84 Ethnikis Antistassos	
	Chalandri	Tel. 01/671 52 93
	15231	Fax. 01/671 87 86
Italy	Abacus Spa	
	Via Carlo Torre 39	Tel. 02/89 40 36 44
	20143 Milano	Fax. 02/58 10 40 69
	ASM SRL	
	Via Olmetto No. 1	Tel. 02/805 39 57
	00191 Roma	Fax. 02/805 55 69
Japan	Japan Market Research Bureau	
	2-13-2 Kami-Osaki	
	Shinagawa-Ku	Tel. 03/3449 8711
	Tokyo 141	Fax. 03/3473 4029
	Nippon Research Centre	
	Daini-Nagapka Building	
	2-8-5 Hatchbori Chuo-Ku	Tel. 03/3552 2415
	Tokyo 104	Fax. 03/3553 0024
Netherlands	NIPO BV	
	Barentszplein 7	Tel. 020/523 84 44
	1013 NJ Amsterdam	Fax. 020/526 43 75

Norway	Scan-Fact A/S	
	Kongens Gate 15	Tel. 02/11 10 54
	Oslo 1	Fax. 02/20 73 98
Portugal	Norma	
	Av 5 de Outubro 122–8	Tel. 1/76 76 04–08
	1000 Lisbon	Fax. 02/20 73 98
Spain	Sofemasa	
	Princesa 1 Torre	Tel. 1/248 96 08
	Madrid 10–6	Fax. 1/547 27 97
Sweden	Burke Marketing Information	
	Box 140 93 (Molndalsvagen 24)	Tel. 031/635 39 00
	400 20 Gothenburg	Fax. 031/40 32 55
Switzerland	Demoscope Marktforschungsinstitut AG	
	Klusenstrasse 17/18	Tel. 041/30 11 88
	6043 Adligenswil	Fax. 041/31 62 94
UK	The Harris Research Centre	
	Holbrooke House	
	34–38 The Rise	
	Richmond	Tel. 0181 332 9898
	Surrey TW10 6UA	Fax. 0181 948 8335
	Taylor Nelson	
	44–46 Upper High Street	
	Epsom	Tel. 01372 729 688
	Surrey KT17 4QS	Fax. 01372 744 100
USA	Louis Harris & Associates	
	630 Fifth Avenue	
	New York 10111	Tel. 212/698 9600
	New York	Fax. 212/698 9559
	Yankelovich Clancy Shulman	
	8 Wright Street	
	Westport	Tel. 203/227 2700
	CT 05880	Fax. 203/454 2109

RESEARCH ASSOCIATIONS

UK   The Market Research Society (MRS)
              15 Northburgh Street   Tel. 0171 490 4911
              London EC1V 0AH   Fax. 0171 490 0608

Europe   European Society for Opinion
              Marketing Research (ESOMAR)
              J.J. Viottastraat 29
              1071 JP Amsterdam   Tel. 31/20 664 2141
              Netherlands   Fax. 31/20 664 2922

USA   Council of American Survey
              Research Organizations (CASPRO)
              3 Upper Devon
              Belle Terre
              Port Jefferson   Tel. 516/928 6954
              New York 11777   Fax. 516/928 8241

Appendix B

Customer segmentation matrices

The following customer segmentation matrices should be completed for every customer or customer grouping (customers that have the same set of product, service and relationship needs).

These matrices cover all the areas associated with *delighting customers* programmes. The completion of the matrices are described in detail in Step 4 (page 78).

Customer:	**x** (of n)	**Segmentation Matrix 1**										

Customer / Product Details

Way to Market: Direct End User / Distributor / Distributor End User
Opinion Shaper - external / internal **(select one only)**

Product Lines	1	2	3	4	5	6	7	8	9	-	-	n
Customer Type (Tick one only)												
User Purchaser / User Opinion Shaper												
Customer Interaction (Tick those appropriate)												
Product / Service Relationship Strategic												
Product Lifecycle (Tick one only)												
Introduction Growth Maturity / Saturation Decline												
Product Growth / Share (Tick one only)												
Market Leader New Products Cash Cows Non-Profitable Products												
Product Strategy (Tick one only)												
Market Penetration Market Extension Product Development Diversification												

Figure B.1 Segmentation matrices.
(a) Customer/product details.

Customer: x (of n)	Segmentation Matrix 2											
Product & Service Attributes												
Way to Market: Direct End User / Distributor / Distributor End User Opinion Shaper - external / internal **(select one only)**												
Product Lines	1	2	3	4	5	6	7	8	9	-	-	n
Service Plane (Tick one only) Plane 1 - n												
Core Product (Tick those appropriate) Attribute 1 to n												
Expected Product (Tick those appropriate) Attribute 1 to n												
Augmented Product (Tick those appropriate) Attribute 1 to n												
Potential Product (Tick those appropriate) Attribute 1 to n												

Figure B.1 continued.
(b) Product and service attributes.

| Customer: | x (of n) | Segmentation Matrix | 3 |

Success Criteria / Communications Activities

Way to Market: Direct End User / Distributor / Distributor End User
Opinion Shaper - external / internal **(select one only)**

Product Lines	1	2	3	4	5	6	7	8	9	-	-	n
Opportunity Details (Tick one only)												
Increase Business												
Increase Customer Loyalty												
Develop Competitive Barrier												
Success Criteria (Tick those appropriate)												
Criteria 1												
2												
3												
4												
5												
6												
7												
8												
9												
-												
n												
Communication Activities (Tick those appropriate)												
Activity 1												
2												
3												
4												
5												
6												
7												
8												
9												
-												
n												

Figure B.1 continued.
(c) Success criteria/communications activities.

Customer: x (of n)	Segmentation Matrix 4

Customer (Survey) Feedback

Way to Market: Direct End User / Distributor / Distributor End User
Opinion Shaper - external / internal **(select one only)**

Product Lines	1	2	3	4	5	6	7	8	9	-	-	n
Customer Feedback (Tick those appropriate)												
Strategic Level: Face to Face Customer Meeting Product / Company Event												
Relationship Level: Face to Face Telephone Survey Postal Survey Customer Meeting User Group Event Focus Group Product / Company Event												
Product / Service Level: Face to Face Telephone Survey Postal Survey Report Card Customer Meeting User Group Event Focus Group Product / Company Event												
Survey Type (Tick those appropriate)												
Tracking Survey: once per year > once per year Event Driven Survey												

Figure B.1 continued.
(d) Customer (survey) feedback.

Appendix C

Questionnaire examples

The following four questionnaires provide a very good example of the types of questions that are asked of different customer types. The examples shown are from IBM UK's Customer Satisfaction Programme. Customer types are discussed in more detail in Step 4 (page 78).

The first questionnaire (Figure C.1) focuses on the relationship aspects and is targeted at the executives and the senior management team in the customer's organization. The next three questionnaires focus on the different customer types involved in the sales channels and are targeted at key decision makers and influencers.

The focus of the second questionnaire (Figure C.2) is on direct sales to customers, while the third questionnaire (Figure C.3) focuses on end user customers that have purchased products and services via agents or distributors. The last survey (Figure C.4) is focused on customers that purchase IBM's products as a key component or for use in their own products.

As can be seen from this set of questionnaires, the customer loyalty questions (overall satisfaction, etc.) are common throughout. The other questions are designed to capture views on the areas most relevant (important) for the customer type concerned.

Your overall view of IBM

- -

1. Overall, how satisfied are you with IBM as a company to do business with?

Very satisfied	Satisfied	Neither satisfied nor dissatisfied	Dissatisfied	Very dissatisfied
☐	☐	☐	☐	☐

Comments and suggestions for improvements:_____
_____
_____
_____

2. How do you rate IBM compared to all other suppliers you deal with?

The best	Above average	Average	Below average	The worst
☐	☐	☐	☐	☐

Comments and suggestions for improvements:_____
_____
_____
_____

3. How satisfied are you with the value received from your investment in our products and services?

Very satisfied	Satisfied	Neither satisfied nor dissatisfied	Dissatisfied	Very dissatisfied	No experience
☐	☐	☐	☐	☐	☐

Comments and suggestions for improvements:_____
_____
_____
_____

Please indicate you satisfaction with the following three aspects of your main IBM contacts:

4. Their knowledge of you and your industry?

Very satisfied	Satisfied	Neither satisfied nor dissatisfied	Dissatisfied	Very dissatisfied	No experience
☐	☐	☐	☐	☐	☐

Comments and suggestions for improvements:_____
_____
_____
_____

5. Their ability to combine products and services into solutions which meet your needs?

Very satisfied	Satisfied	Neither satisfied nor dissatisfied	Dissatisfied	Very dissatisfied	No experience
☐	☐	☐	☐	☐	☐

Comments and suggestions for improvements:_____
_____
_____
_____

6. Their responsiveness to your needs and requests?

Very satisfied	Satisfied	Neither satisfied nor dissatisfied	Dissatisfied	Very dissatisfied	No experience
☐	☐	☐	☐	☐	☐

Comments and suggestions for improvements:_____
_____
_____
_____

Figure C.1 Questionnaire focusing relationship.

Your overall view of IBM

7. **How satisfied are you with the quality of our products and services?**

Very satisfied	Satisfied	Neither satisfied nor dissatisfied	Dissatisfied	Very dissatisfied	No experience
☐	☐	☐	☐	☐	☐

Comments and suggestions for improvements:_____

_____

8. **How satisfied are you with our after sales support?**

Very satisfied	Satisfied	Neither satisfied nor dissatisfied	Dissatisfied	Very dissatisfied	No experience
☐	☐	☐	☐	☐	☐

Comments and suggestions for improvements:_____

_____

9. **How satisfied are you with the ease of doing business with us?**

Very satisfied	Satisfied	Neither satisfied nor dissatisfied	Dissatisfied	Very dissatisfied	No experience
☐	☐	☐	☐	☐	☐

Comments and suggestions for improvements:_____

_____

10. **How satisfied are you with:**

	Very satisfied	Satisfied	Neither satisfied nor dissatisfied	Dissatisfied	Very dissatisfied	No experience
The commitments we make to you?	☐	☐	☐	☐	☐	☐
The extent to which we meet them?	☐	☐	☐	☐	☐	☐

Comments and suggestions for improvements:_____

_____

Please comment on what you consider to be the most NEGATIVE aspects of your dealings with us.

_____

_____

Please comment on what you consider to be the most POSITIVE aspects of your dealings with us.

_____

_____

Please tell us about any other topics that are important to you that you would like us to include in this questionnaire.

_____

_____

Figure C.1 continued.

Identity

Please complete the relevant sections below if you are not the individual to whom this survey was addressed or if the details of your organisation, as shown on the address label, are incorrect in any way.

NAME _____

TITLE _____

ORGANISATION _____

ADDRESS _____

_____

_____

_____

If you do **not** wish the comments you have made to be passed to your IBM office for action, but prefer to remain anonymous, please tick the box below.

☐

Thank you for completing this questionnaire.

Please use the attached reply paid envelope to return it to:

GSR Group Ltd, 361-373 City Road, London, EC1V 1JJ, who have been commissioned by us to manage this survey.

Figure C.1 continued.

Your overall view of IBM

1. **Overall, how satisfied are you with IBM as a company to do business with?**

Very satisfied	Satisfied	Neither satisfied nor dissatisfied	Dissatisfied	Very dissatisfied
☐	☐	☐	☐	☐

Comments and suggestions for improvements:_____

2. **How do you rate IBM compared to all other suppliers you deal with?**

The best	Above average	Average	Below average	The worst
☐	☐	☐	☐	☐

Comments and suggestions for improvements:_____

3. **How satisfied are you with the value received from your investment in our products and services?**

Very satisfied	Satisfied	Neither satisfied nor dissatisfied	Dissatisfied	Very dissatisfied	No experience
☐	☐	☐	☐	☐	☐

Comments and suggestions for improvements:_____

4. **How satisfied are you with the support provided by your main contact(s)?**

Very satisfied	Satisfied	Neither satisfied nor dissatisfied	Dissatisfied	Very dissatisfied	No experience
☐	☐	☐	☐	☐	☐

Comments and suggestions for improvements:_____

5. **How satisfied are you with the quality of our products and services?**

Very satisfied	Satisfied	Neither satisfied nor dissatisfied	Dissatisfied	Very dissatisfied	No experience
☐	☐	☐	☐	☐	☐

Comments and suggestions for improvements:_____

6. **How satisfied are you with our implementation, operational and maintenance support?**

Very satisfied	Satisfied	Neither satisfied nor dissatisfied	Dissatisfied	Very dissatisfied	No experience
☐	☐	☐	☐	☐	☐

Comments and suggestions for improvements:_____

Figure C.2 Questionnaire focusing direct slaes.

Your overall view of IBM

7. **How satisfied are you with the clarity and simplicity of our contract terms and contracting procedures?**

Very satisfied	Satisfied	Neither satisfied nor dissatisfied	Dissatisfied	Very dissatisfied	No experience
☐	☐	☐	☐	☐	☐

Comments and suggestions for improvements:_____

_____

_____

8. **How satisfied are you with the ease of doing business with us?**

Very satisfied	Satisfied	Neither satisfied nor dissatisfied	Dissatisfied	Very dissatisfied	No experience
☐	☐	☐	☐	☐	☐

Comments and suggestions for improvements:_____

_____

_____

9. **How satisfied are you with:**

	Very satisfied	Satisfied	Neither satisfied nor dissatisfied	Dissatisfied	Very dissatisfied	No experience
The commitments we make to you?	☐	☐	☐	☐	☐	☐
The extent to which we meet them?	☐	☐	☐	☐	☐	☐

Comments and suggestions for improvements:_____

_____

_____

10. **How satisfied are you with the way we handle the following:**

	Very satisfied	Satisfied	Neither satisfied nor dissatisfied	Dissatisfied	Very dissatisfied	No experience
Telephone communications?	☐	☐	☐	☐	☐	☐
Written communications?	☐	☐	☐	☐	☐	☐

Comments and suggestions for improvements:_____

_____

_____

Thank you for completing this important section of the questionnaire.

We would also appreciate opinions and comments on the sections that follow.

Figure C.2 continued.

Sales support

Please indicate your satisfaction with the following aspects of our sales support:

11. Our knowledge of you and your industry?

Very satisfied	Satisfied	Neither satisfied nor dissatisfied	Dissatisfied	Very dissatisfied	No experience
☐	☐	☐	☐	☐	☐

Comments and suggestions for improvements:_____

_____

_____

12. Our knowledge of your I/S strategy, objectives and applications?

Very satisfied	Satisfied	Neither satisfied nor dissatisfied	Dissatisfied	Very dissatisfied	No experience
☐	☐	☐	☐	☐	☐

Comments and suggestions for improvements:_____

_____

_____

13. Our knowledge of our products and services?

Very satisfied	Satisfied	Neither satisfied nor dissatisfied	Dissatisfied	Very dissatisfied	No experience
☐	☐	☐	☐	☐	☐

Comments and suggestions for improvements:_____

_____

_____

14. Our ability to combine products and services into solutions which meet your needs?

Very satisfied	Satisfied	Neither satisfied nor dissatisfied	Dissatisfied	Very dissatisfied	No experience
☐	☐	☐	☐	☐	☐

Comments and suggestions for improvements:_____

_____

_____

15. Our responsiveness to your needs and requests?

Very satisfied	Satisfied	Neither satisfied nor dissatisfied	Dissatisfied	Very dissatisfied	No experience
☐	☐	☐	☐	☐	☐

Comments and suggestions for improvements:_____

_____

_____

16. Our ability to provide support on an International basis?

Very satisfied	Satisfied	Neither satisfied nor dissatisfied	Dissatisfied	Very dissatisfied	No experience
☐	☐	☐	☐	☐	☐

Comments and suggestions for improvements:_____

_____

_____

Figure C.2 continued.

Sales support

---

17. The continuity of your main sales contacts?

	Very satisfied	Satisfied	Neither satisfied nor dissatisfied	Dissatisfied	Very dissatisfied	No experience
	☐	☐	☐	☐	☐	☐

Comments and suggestions for improvements:_____

_____

_____

_____

Products and services

Information

---

18. How satisfied are you with the way we keep you informed about our products and services?

	Very satisfied	Satisfied	Neither satisfied nor dissatisfied	Dissatisfied	Very dissatisfied	No experience
	☐	☐	☐	☐	☐	☐

Comments and suggestions for improvements:_____

_____

_____

_____

Hardware

---

19. How satisfied are you with the following IBM hardware products?

	Very satisfied	Satisfied	Neither satisfied nor dissatisfied	Dissatisfied	Very dissatisfied	No experience
Processors	☐	☐	☐	☐	☐	☐
Disks	☐	☐	☐	☐	☐	☐
Tapes	☐	☐	☐	☐	☐	☐
Printers	☐	☐	☐	☐	☐	☐
Personal Systems	☐	☐	☐	☐	☐	☐
Displays	☐	☐	☐	☐	☐	☐
LAN and Networking	☐	☐	☐	☐	☐	☐
Industry terminals (such as EPOS, ATMs etc)	☐	☐	☐	☐	☐	☐

Comments and suggestions for improvements:

We would particularly welcome your comments in the areas of ease of use, reliability, function and documentation.

Product	Area	Comment
_____	_____	_____
_____	_____	_____
_____	_____	_____
_____	_____	_____
_____	_____	_____
_____	_____	_____

Figure C.2 continued.

Products and services

Software

20. How satisfied are you with the following IBM software products?

	Very satisfied	Satisfied	Neither satisfied nor dissatisfied	Dissatisfied	Very dissatisfied	No experience
Operating systems	☐	☐	☐	☐	☐	☐
LAN and Networking	☐	☐	☐	☐	☐	☐
Application software	☐	☐	☐	☐	☐	☐
Application enabling software (*)	☐	☐	☐	☐	☐	☐

(*eg database software such as IMS, DB2 and SQL/DS; transaction processors such as CICS and IMS/TM; languages such as COBOL, RPG and PL/1; AD/Cycle software such as CSP and the AD/Cycle International Alliance software from vendors such as SYNON, Knowledgeware, Easel and Microfocus)

We would particularly welcome your comments in the areas of ease of use, reliability, function and documentation.

Product	Area	Comment
_____	_____	_____
_____	_____	_____
_____	_____	_____
_____	_____	_____

Networking

We provide a wide range of networking hardware and software products. These range from PC adaptors to routers, hubs and corporate network controllers. Together, these products enable you to implement both Local and Wide area networks.

21. Overall, how satisfied are you with your:

	Very satisfied	Satisfied	Neither satisfied nor dissatisfied	Dissatisfied	Very dissatisfied	No experience
Local area networks?	☐	☐	☐	☐	☐	☐
Wide area networks?	☐	☐	☐	☐	☐	☐
Multi-vendor networks?	☐	☐	☐	☐	☐	☐

We would particularly welcome your comments in the areas of ease of use, reliability, function and documentation.

Product	Area	Comment
_____	_____	_____
_____	_____	_____
_____	_____	_____
_____	_____	_____

Consultancy and Services

We provide a wide range of Consultancy and Services. These are delivered in engagements from a few hours to the largest systems integration contracts.

22. How satisfied are you with our Consultancy and Services?

Very satisfied	Satisfied	Neither satisfied nor dissatisfied	Dissatisfied	Very dissatisfied	No experience
☐	☐	☐	☐	☐	☐

We would particularly welcome your comments in the areas of Management, Industry and Quality Consultancy, Project Management, System Design, Application Development, Systems Management, Networking, Open Systems and IT Product Implementataion, all of which we provide. Specific comments on all aspects are valuable, particularly on the skills of our people, the way we work with you and the quality and timeliness of what we deliver.

Product	Area	Comment
_____	_____	_____
_____	_____	_____
_____	_____	_____
_____	_____	_____

Figure C.2 continued.

Customer Service

As well as the familiar maintenance role, Customer Service offers a wide range of hardware and software and operational services to assist you in running a cost-effective IT operation.

Please indicate the major source of maintenance for your IBM hardware.	☐ 1 IBM Maintenance contract ☐ 2 IBM Per Call ☐ 3 Maintained by an organisation other than IBM ☐ 4 Self-maintained

If you have answered 3 or 4 please go to question 27.

How satisfied are you with:

23. Our speed of response to your hardware service calls (that is, from the time the problem is reported until the Customer Engineer starts to work on it)?

Very satisfied	Satisfied	Neither satisfied nor dissatisfied	Dissatisfied	Very dissatisfied	No experience
☐	☐	☐	☐	☐	☐

Comments and suggestions for improvements:_____

_____

_____

24. The hardware maintenance services provided to your central site?

Very satisfied	Satisfied	Neither satisfied nor dissatisfied	Dissatisfied	Very dissatisfied	No experience
☐	☐	☐	☐	☐	☐

Comments and suggestions for improvements:_____

_____

_____

25. The maintenance services provided to your printers?

Very satisfied	Satisfied	Neither satisfied nor dissatisfied	Dissatisfied	Very dissatisfied	No experience
☐	☐	☐	☐	☐	☐

We now have a specialist maintenance organisation dedicated to printers.

Comments and suggestions for improvements:_____

_____

_____

26. Our ability to fix the IBM equipment on your network?

Very satisfied	Satisfied	Neither satisfied nor dissatisfied	Dissatisfied	Very dissatisfied	No experience
☐	☐	☐	☐	☐	☐

Comments and suggestions for improvements:_____

_____

_____

Figure C.2 continued.

Customer Service

27. The service provided by our Software Support Centre in answer to software defect problems?

Very satisfied	Satisfied	Neither satisfied nor dissatisfied	Dissatisfied	Very dissatisfied	No experience
☐	☐	☐	☐	☐	☐

Comments and suggestions for improvements:_____

_____

_____

_____

28. If you have an Operational Support Specialist (OSS) as part of an Operational Support Agreement (OSA), how satisfied are you with the services provided by the OSS?

Very satisfied	Satisfied	Neither satisfied nor dissatisfied	Dissatisfied	Very dissatisfied	No experience
☐	☐	☐	☐	☐	☐

Comments and suggestions for improvements:_____

_____

_____

_____

29. If you use our central query answering facilities (eg ASSIST/400, ES/ASSIST, CALL/AIX, PC HELPWARE or other Helpdesk services), how satisfied are you with the services provided?

Very satisfied	Satisfied	Neither satisfied nor dissatisfied	Dissatisfied	Very dissatisfied	No experience
☐	☐	☐	☐	☐	☐

Comments and suggestions for improvements:

Service	*Comment*
_____	_____
_____	_____
_____	_____

Education

IBM Education services can provide you with a wide spectrum of education and training, encompassing technical, personal and business skills.

30. How satisfied are you with the Education you have received?

Very satisfied	Satisfied	Neither satisfied nor dissatisfied	Dissatisfied	Very dissatisfied	No experience
☐	☐	☐	☐	☐	☐

Comments and suggestions for improvements:_____

_____

_____

_____

Outsourcing

31. How satisfied are you with our Outsourcing (Facilities Management) services?

Very satisfied	Satisfied	Neither satisfied nor dissatisfied	Dissatisfied	Very dissatisfied	No experience
☐	☐	☐	☐	☐	☐

Comments and suggestions for improvements:_____

_____

_____

_____

Figure C.2 continued.

Administrative support

How satisfied are you with:

32. The quality of our product deliveries?

Very satisfied	Satisfied	Neither satisfied nor dissatisfied	Dissatisfied	Very dissatisfied	No experience
☐	☐	☐	☐	☐	☐

This includes delivering hardware and software to match your order specification, meeting the delivery commitments we make, completeness, convenience and packaging/handling.

Comments and suggestions for improvements:_____
_____
_____
_____

33. The quality of the invoices you receive from us?

Very satisfied	Satisfied	Neither satisfied nor dissatisfied	Dissatisfied	Very dissatisfied	No experience
☐	☐	☐	☐	☐	☐

Comments and suggestions for improvements:_____
_____
_____
_____

34. The support you receive from administrative personnel?

Very satisfied	Satisfied	Neither satisfied nor dissatisfied	Dissatisfied	Very dissatisfied	No experience
☐	☐	☐	☐	☐	☐

Comments and suggestions for improvements:_____
_____
_____
_____

Our Business Associate

IBM's Business Associates, Value Added Remarketers and Dealers are third party organisations acting in a marketing capacity either with us or on our behalf. These companies can sell and support almost all of our product range.

35. How satisfied are you with the support provided by this company?

Company name(s)

Very satisfied	Satisfied	Neither satisfied nor dissatisfied	Dissatisfied	Very dissatisfied	No experience
☐	☐	☐	☐	☐	☐
☐	☐	☐	☐	☐	☐
☐	☐	☐	☐	☐	☐
☐	☐	☐	☐	☐	☐

_____
_____
_____
_____

Comments and suggestions for improvements:_____
_____
_____
_____

Figure C.2 continued.

Summary
- -

Please comment on what you consider to be the most NEGATIVE aspects of your dealings with us.

_____
_____
_____
_____
_____
_____

Please comment on what you consider to be the most POSITIVE aspects of your dealings with us.

_____
_____
_____
_____
_____
_____

Please tell us about any other topics that are important to you that you would like us to include in this questionnaire.

_____
_____
_____
_____
_____
_____

Please indicate the likelihood that you would choose us as your supplier for these products and services, if you were deciding today.

	Definitely	Probably	Might or might not	Probably not	Definitely not
Total solution	☐	☐	☐	☐	☐
Consultancy and Services	☐	☐	☐	☐	☐
Hardware	☐	☐	☐	☐	☐
Application software	☐	☐	☐	☐	☐
Maintenance services	☐	☐	☐	☐	☐
Education	☐	☐	☐	☐	☐

If you are unlikely to choose us in any area it would help us to understand your reasons, thank you.

Product/service	Comment
_____	_____
_____	_____
_____	_____
_____	_____
_____	_____
_____	_____
_____	_____

Figure C.2 continued.

Importance

To help us to understand what is important to you, we would be grateful if you would indicate a rating against each of the following topics.

Overall

	Critical	Very important	Of some importance	Largely unimportant	Of no importance
Value from your investment	☐	☐	☐	☐	☐
Support from main contact(s)	☐	☐	☐	☐	☐
Quality of products and services	☐	☐	☐	☐	☐
After sales support	☐	☐	☐	☐	☐
Contract terms and procedures	☐	☐	☐	☐	☐
Ease of doing business	☐	☐	☐	☐	☐
Making commitments	☐	☐	☐	☐	☐
Meeting commitments	☐	☐	☐	☐	☐
Telephone communications	☐	☐	☐	☐	☐
Written communications	☐	☐	☐	☐	☐

Sales support

	Critical	Very important	Of some importance	Largely unimportant	Of no importance
Knowledge of you and your industry	☐	☐	☐	☐	☐
Knowledge of your strategy	☐	☐	☐	☐	☐
Knowledge of our products and services	☐	☐	☐	☐	☐
Combine products and services into solutions	☐	☐	☐	☐	☐
Responsiveness	☐	☐	☐	☐	☐
International support	☐	☐	☐	☐	☐
Continuity	☐	☐	☐	☐	☐

Products and services

	Critical	Very important	Of some importance	Largely unimportant	Of no importance
Keeping you informed	☐	☐	☐	☐	☐
Quality of hardware	☐	☐	☐	☐	☐
Quality of Operating systems	☐	☐	☐	☐	☐
Quality of LAN and Networking software	☐	☐	☐	☐	☐
Quality of Application software	☐	☐	☐	☐	☐
Quality of Application enabling software	☐	☐	☐	☐	☐
Local area networks	☐	☐	☐	☐	☐
Wide area networks	☐	☐	☐	☐	☐
Multi-vendor networks	☐	☐	☐	☐	☐
Consultancy and Services	☐	☐	☐	☐	☐
Speed of response to service calls	☐	☐	☐	☐	☐
Hardware maintenance service	☐	☐	☐	☐	☐
Printer maintenance service	☐	☐	☐	☐	☐
Ability to fix your network equipment	☐	☐	☐	☐	☐
Software Support Centre	☐	☐	☐	☐	☐
Operational Support Specialist service	☐	☐	☐	☐	☐
Central query facilities	☐	☐	☐	☐	☐
Education	☐	☐	☐	☐	☐
Outsourcing	☐	☐	☐	☐	☐

Figure C.2 continued.

Importance

	Critical	Very important	Of some importance	Largely unimportant	Of no importance
Administrative support					
Quality of product deliveries	☐	☐	☐	☐	☐
Quality of invoices	☐	☐	☐	☐	☐
Administrative personnel	☐	☐	☐	☐	☐
Business Associates	☐	☐	☐	☐	☐

Identity

Please complete the relevant sections below if you are not the individual to whom this survey was addressed or if the details of your organisation, as shown on the address label, are incorrect in any way.

NAME _____

TITLE _____

ORGANISATION _____

ADDRESS _____

_____

_____

_____

If you do **not** wish the comments you have made to be passed to your IBM office for action, but prefer to remain anonymous, please tick the box below.

☐

Thank you for completing this questionnaire.

Please use the attached reply paid envelope to return it to:

GSR Group Ltd, 361-373 City Road, London, EC1V 1JJ, who have been commissioned by us to manage this survey.

Figure C.2 continued.

Your overall view of IBM and your Business Associate

1. How satisfied are you with the value received from your investment in our products and services?

Very satisfied	Satisfied	Neither satisfied nor dissatisfied	Dissatisfied	Very dissatisfied	No experience
☐	☐	☐	☐	☐	☐

Comments and suggestions for improvements:_____

_____

_____

_____

2. How do you rate IBM compared to all other suppliers you deal with?

The best	Above average	Average	Below average	The worst
☐	☐	☐	☐	☐

Comments and suggestions for improvements:_____

_____

_____

_____

3. How satisfied are you with the quality of our products and services?

Very satisfied	Satisfied	Neither satisfied nor dissatisfied	Dissatisfied	Very dissatisfied	No experience
☐	☐	☐	☐	☐	☐

Comments and suggestions for improvements:_____

_____

_____

_____

4. How satisfied are you with our implementation, operational and maintenance support?

Very satisfied	Satisfied	Neither satisfied nor dissatisfied	Dissatisfied	Very dissatisfied	No experience
☐	☐	☐	☐	☐	☐

Comments and suggestions for improvements:_____

_____

_____

_____

5. Considering all aspects of IBM's products and services, how satisfied are you overall?

Very satisfied	Satisfied	Neither satisfied nor dissatisfied	Dissatisfied	Very dissatisfied
☐	☐	☐	☐	☐

Comments and suggestions for improvements:_____

_____

_____

_____

6. Overall, how satisfied are you with your Business Associate as a company to do business with?

Very satisfied	Satisfied	Neither satisfied nor dissatisfied	Dissatisfied	Very dissatisfied
☐	☐	☐	☐	☐

Comments and suggestions for improvements:_____

_____

_____

_____

Thank you for completing this important section of the questionnaire.

We would also appreciate opinions and comments on the sections that follow.

Figure C.3 Questionnaire focusing sales via agents or distributors.

Your Business Associate

The following questions refer to your satisfaction with your Business Associate.

Marketing support

How satisfied are you with:

7. Their ability to understand your business?

Very satisfied	Satisfied	Neither satisfied nor dissatisfied	Dissatisfied	Very dissatisfied	No experience
☐	☐	☐	☐	☐	☐

Comments and suggestions for improvements:_____

_____

_____

_____

8. The way they keep you informed about IBM's products and services?

Very satisfied	Satisfied	Neither satisfied nor dissatisfied	Dissatisfied	Very dissatisfied	No experience
☐	☐	☐	☐	☐	☐

Comments and suggestions for improvements:_____

_____

_____

_____

9. Their level of knowledge of IBM's products and and services?

Very satisfied	Satisfied	Neither satisfied nor dissatisfied	Dissatisfied	Very dissatisfied	No experience
☐	☐	☐	☐	☐	☐

Comments and suggestions for improvements:_____

_____

_____

_____

10. Their ability to combine products and services into solutions which meet your needs?

Very satisfied	Satisfied	Neither satisfied nor dissatisfied	Dissatisfied	Very dissatisfied	No experience
☐	☐	☐	☐	☐	☐

Comments and suggestions for improvements:_____

_____

_____

_____

11. The frequency of their contact to discuss IBM's products and services?

Very satisfied	Satisfied	Neither satisfied nor dissatisfied	Dissatisfied	Very dissatisfied	No experience
☐	☐	☐	☐	☐	☐

Comments and suggestions for improvements:_____

_____

_____

_____

12. Their ability to respond speedily and effectively should you experience any problems?

Very satisfied	Satisfied	Neither satisfied nor dissatisfied	Dissatisfied	Very dissatisfied	No experience
☐	☐	☐	☐	☐	☐

Comments and suggestions for improvements:_____

_____

_____

_____

Figure C.3 continued.

Products and services

Application software

13. How satisfied are you with:

	Very satisfied	Satisfied	Neither satisfied nor dissatisfied	Dissatisfied	Very dissatisfied	No experience
Their application software?	☐	☐	☐	☐	☐	☐
Their ability to keep you informed of appropriate application software?	☐	☐	☐	☐	☐	☐

Comments and suggestions for improvements:_____

Technical support

Your Business Associate may provide you with "Hotline" support offering guidance and assistance in managing your IBM system.

14. How satisfied are you with this support?

	Very satisfied	Satisfied	Neither satisfied nor dissatisfied	Dissatisfied	Very dissatisfied	No experience
	☐	☐	☐	☐	☐	☐

Comments and suggestions for improvements:_____

Education

Business Associates may provide a range of courses to help you use our systems effectively.

15. How satisfied are you with the education that you have received?

	Very satisfied	Satisfied	Neither satisfied nor dissatisfied	Dissatisfied	Very dissatisfied	No experience
	☐	☐	☐	☐	☐	☐

Comments and suggestions for improvements:_____

Administrative support

16. How satisfied are you with your Business Associate's handling of your:

	Very satisfied	Satisfied	Neither satisfied nor dissatisfied	Dissatisfied	Very dissatisfied	No experience
Written communications?	☐	☐	☐	☐	☐	☐
Telephone communications?	☐	☐	☐	☐	☐	☐

Comments and suggestions for improvements:_____

Figure C.3 continued.

IBM

The following questions refer to your satisfaction with IBM.

Products and services

Hardware

17. How satisfied are you with the following IBM hardware products?

	Very satisfied	Satisfied	Neither satisfied nor dissatisfied	Dissatisfied	Very dissatisfied	No experience
Processors	☐	☐	☐	☐	☐	☐
Disks	☐	☐	☐	☐	☐	☐
Tapes	☐	☐	☐	☐	☐	☐
Printers	☐	☐	☐	☐	☐	☐
Personal Systems	☐	☐	☐	☐	☐	☐
Displays	☐	☐	☐	☐	☐	☐
LAN and Networking	☐	☐	☐	☐	☐	☐
Industry terminals (such as EPOS, ATMs etc)	☐	☐	☐	☐	☐	☐

Comments and suggestions for improvements:

We would particularly welcome your comments in the areas of ease of use, reliability, function and documentation.

Product	Area	Comment

Software

18. How satisfied are you with the following IBM software products?

	Very satisfied	Satisfied	Neither satisfied nor dissatisfied	Dissatisfied	Very dissatisfied	No experience
Operating systems	☐	☐	☐	☐	☐	☐
LAN and Networking	☐	☐	☐	☐	☐	☐
Application software (eg Office)	☐	☐	☐	☐	☐	☐
Application enabling software (eg Query)	☐	☐	☐	☐	☐	☐

Comments and suggestions for improvements:

We would particularly welcome your comments in the areas of ease of use, reliability, function and documentation.

Product	Area	Comment

Figure C.3 continued.

Consultancy and Services

IBM provides a wide range of Consultancy and Services. These are delivered in engagements from a few hours to the largest systems integration contracts.

19. How satisfied are you with our Consultancy and Services?

Very satisfied	Satisfied	Neither satisfied nor dissatisfied	Dissatisfied	Very dissatisfied	No experience
☐	☐	☐	☐	☐	☐

We would particularly welcome your comments in the areas of Management, Industry and Quality Consultancy, Project Management, System Design, Application Development, Systems Management, Networking, Open Systems and IT Project Implementation, all of which we provide. Specific comments on all aspects are valuable, particularly on the skills of our people, the way we work with you and the quality and timeliness of what we deliver.

Area	*Comment*
_____	_____
_____	_____
_____	_____
_____	_____

Customer Service

As well as the familiar maintenance role, IBM Customer Service offers a wide range of hardware and software services to assist you in running a cost-effective IT operation.

Please indicate the major source of maintenance for your IBM hardware.

☐ 1   IBM Maintenance contract
☐ 2   IBM Per Call
☐ 3   Maintained by an organisation other than IBM
☐ 4   Self-maintained

If you have answered 3 or 4 above please go to question 24.

How satisfied are you with:

20. Our speed of response to your hardware service calls (that is, from the time the problem is reported until the Customer Engineer starts to work on it)?

Very satisfied	Satisfied	Neither satisfied nor dissatisfied	Dissatisfied	Very dissatisfied	No experience
☐	☐	☐	☐	☐	☐

Comments and suggestions for improvements:_____
_____
_____
_____

21. The hardware maintenance services provided to your central site?

Very satisfied	Satisfied	Neither satisfied nor dissatisfied	Dissatisfied	Very dissatisfied	No experience
☐	☐	☐	☐	☐	☐

Comments and suggestions for improvements:_____
_____
_____
_____

Figure C.3 continued.

Customer Service

- -

**22. The maintenance service provided to
your printers?**

Very satisfied	Satisfied	Neither satisfied nor dissatisfied	Dissatisfied	Very dissatisfied	No experience
☐	☐	☐	☐	☐	☐

We now have a specialist maintenance organisation dedicated to printers.

Comments and suggestions for improvements:_____
_____
_____
_____

23. Our ability to fix the IBM equipment on your network?

Very satisfied	Satisfied	Neither satisfied nor dissatisfied	Dissatisfied	Very dissatisfied	No experience
☐	☐	☐	☐	☐	☐

Comments and suggestions for improvements:_____
_____
_____
_____

**24. The service provided by our Software Support
Centre in answer to software defect problems?**

Very satisfied	Satisfied	Neither satisfied nor dissatisfied	Dissatisfied	Very dissatisfied	No experience
☐	☐	☐	☐	☐	☐

Comments and suggestions for improvements:_____
_____
_____
_____

Education

- -

IBM Education Services can provide you with a wide spectrum of education and training, encompassing technical, personal and business skills.

**25. How satisfied are you with the education that you
have received?**

Very satisfied	Satisfied	Neither satisfied nor dissatisfied	Dissatisfied	Very dissatisfied	No experience
☐	☐	☐	☐	☐	☐

Comments and suggestions for improvements:_____
_____
_____
_____

Figure C.3 continued.

Administrative support

_ _

How satisfied are you with:

26. IBM's handling of your:

	Very satisfied	Satisfied	Neither satisfied nor dissatisfied	Dissatisfied	Very dissatisfied	No experience
Written communications?	☐	☐	☐	☐	☐	☐
Telephone communications?	☐	☐	☐	☐	☐	☐

Comments and suggestions for improvements:_____

_____

_____

_____

27. The quality of our product deliveries?

	Very satisfied	Satisfied	Neither satisfied nor dissatisfied	Dissatisfied	Very dissatisfied	No experience
	☐	☐	☐	☐	☐	☐

This includes delivering hardware and software to match your order specification, meeting the delivery commitments we make, completeness, convenience and packaging/handling.

Comments and suggestions for improvements:_____

_____

_____

_____

28. The quality of the invoices you receive from us?

	Very satisfied	Satisfied	Neither satisfied nor dissatisfied	Dissatisfied	Very dissatisfied	No experience
	☐	☐	☐	☐	☐	☐

Comments and suggestions for improvements:_____

_____

_____

_____

29. The support you receive from administrative personnel?

	Very satisfied	Satisfied	Neither satisfied nor dissatisfied	Dissatisfied	Very dissatisfied	No experience
	☐	☐	☐	☐	☐	☐

Comments and suggestions for improvements:_____

_____

_____

_____

Figure C.3 continued.

Summary
_____

Please comment on what you consider to be the most NEGATIVE aspects of your dealings with IBM and your Business Associate.

IBM_____

_____

_____

_____

BUSINESS ASSOCIATE _____

_____

_____

_____

Please comment on what you consider to be the most POSITIVE aspects of your dealings with IBM and your Business Associate.

IBM _____

_____

_____

_____

BUSINESS ASSOCIATE _____

_____

_____

_____

Please tell us about any other topics that are important to you that you would like us to include in this questionnaire.

_____

_____

_____

_____

Please indicate the likelihood that you would choose IBM or your Business Associate as your supplier for these products and services, if you were deciding today.

	Definitely	Probably	Might or might not	Probably not	Definitely not
Total solution	☐	☐	☐	☐	☐
Hardware	☐	☐	☐	☐	☐
Application software	☐	☐	☐	☐	☐
Maintenance services	☐	☐	☐	☐	☐
Education	☐	☐	☐	☐	☐

If you are unlikely to choose us in any area it would help us to understand your reasons, thank you.

Product/service	Comment
_____	_____
_____	_____
_____	_____
_____	_____
_____	_____
_____	_____
_____	_____

Figure C.3 continued.

Importance

To help us to understand what is important to you, we would be grateful if you would indicate a rating against each of the following topics.

	Critical	Very important	Of some importance	Largely unimportant	Of no importance

IBM and your Business Associate

Value from your investment ☐ ☐ ☐ ☐ ☐

Quality of products and services ☐ ☐ ☐ ☐ ☐

After sales support ☐ ☐ ☐ ☐ ☐

Your Business Associate

Understand your business ☐ ☐ ☐ ☐ ☐

Information about products and services ☐ ☐ ☐ ☐ ☐

Knowledge of IBM's products and services ☐ ☐ ☐ ☐ ☐

Combine products and services into solutions ☐ ☐ ☐ ☐ ☐

Frequency of contact ☐ ☐ ☐ ☐ ☐

Responsiveness ☐ ☐ ☐ ☐ ☐

Application software ☐ ☐ ☐ ☐ ☐

Information about Application software ☐ ☐ ☐ ☐ ☐

Technical Support ☐ ☐ ☐ ☐ ☐

Education ☐ ☐ ☐ ☐ ☐

Written communications ☐ ☐ ☐ ☐ ☐

Telephone communications ☐ ☐ ☐ ☐ ☐

IBM

Quality of hardware ☐ ☐ ☐ ☐ ☐

Quality of Operating systems ☐ ☐ ☐ ☐ ☐

Quality of LAN and Networking software ☐ ☐ ☐ ☐ ☐

Quality of Application software ☐ ☐ ☐ ☐ ☐

Quality of Application enabling software ☐ ☐ ☐ ☐ ☐

Consultancy and Services ☐ ☐ ☐ ☐ ☐

Speed of response to service calls ☐ ☐ ☐ ☐ ☐

Hardware maintenance service ☐ ☐ ☐ ☐ ☐

Printer maintenance service ☐ ☐ ☐ ☐ ☐

Ability to fix your network equipment ☐ ☐ ☐ ☐ ☐

Software Support Centre ☐ ☐ ☐ ☐ ☐

Education ☐ ☐ ☐ ☐ ☐

Written communications ☐ ☐ ☐ ☐ ☐

Telephone communications ☐ ☐ ☐ ☐ ☐

Quality of product deliveries ☐ ☐ ☐ ☐ ☐

Quality of invoices ☐ ☐ ☐ ☐ ☐

Administrative personnel ☐ ☐ ☐ ☐ ☐

Figure C.3 continued.

Identity

Please complete the relevant sections below if you are not the individual to whom this survey was addressed or if the details of your organisation, as shown on the address label, are incorrect in any way.

NAME _____

TITLE _____

ORGANISATION _____

ADDRESS _____

_____

_____

_____

If you do **not** wish the comments you have made to be passed to your IBM office for action, but prefer to remain anonymous, please tick the box below.

☐

Thank you for completing this questionnaire.

Please use the attached reply paid envelope to return it to:

GSR Group Ltd, 361-373 City Road, London, EC1V 1JJ, who have been commissioned by us to manage this survey.

Figure C.3 continued.

Your overall view of IBM and your Business Associate

1. How satisfied are you with the value received
from your investment in our products and services?

Very satisfied	Satisfied	Neither satisfied nor dissatisfied	Dissatisfied	Very dissatisfied	No experience
☐	☐	☐	☐	☐	☐

Comments and suggestions for improvements:_____

_____

_____

2. How satisfied are you with the quality of our
products and services?

Very satisfied	Satisfied	Neither satisfied nor dissatisfied	Dissatisfied	Very dissatisfied	No experience
☐	☐	☐	☐	☐	☐

Comments and suggestions for improvements:_____

_____

_____

3. How satisfied are you with our implementation,
operational and maintenance support?

Very satisfied	Satisfied	Neither satisfied nor dissatisfied	Dissatisfied	Very dissatisfied	No experience
☐	☐	☐	☐	☐	☐

Comments and suggestions for improvements:_____

_____

_____

4. Considering all aspects of IBM's products and services,
how satisfied are you overall?

Very satisfied	Satisfied	Neither satisfied nor dissatisfied	Dissatisfied	Very dissatisfied
☐	☐	☐	☐	☐

Comments and suggestions for improvements:_____

_____

_____

Name of your principal Business Associate _____

5. Overall, how satisfied are you with your principal RISC
System/6000 Business Associate as a company to do
business with?

Very satisfied	Satisfied	Neither satisfied nor dissatisfied	Dissatisfied	Very dissatisfied
☐	☐	☐	☐	☐

Comments and suggestions for improvements:_____

_____

_____

6. How long has this Business Associate supported your
installation?

Less than 3 months	3 - 6 Months	7 - 12 Months	1-2 Years	More than 2 years
☐	☐	☐	☐	☐

Comments and suggestions for improvements:_____

_____

_____

Thank you for completing this important section of the questionnaire.

We would also appreciate opinions and comments on the sections that follow.

Figure C.4 Questionnaire focusing on key component purchasers.

Your Business Associate

The following questions refer to your satisfaction with your Business Associate.

Marketing support

How satisfied are you with:

7. Their ability to understand your business?

Very satisfied	Satisfied	Neither satisfied nor dissatisfied	Dissatisfied	Very dissatisfied	No experience
☐	☐	☐	☐	☐	☐

Comments and suggestions for improvements:_____

_____

_____

_____

8. Their level of knowledge of the RISC System/6000 hardware and software product ranges?

Very satisfied	Satisfied	Neither satisfied nor dissatisfied	Dissatisfied	Very dissatisfied	No experience
☐	☐	☐	☐	☐	☐

Comments and suggestions for improvements:_____

_____

_____

_____

9. Their ability to combine products and services into solutions which meet your needs?

Very satisfied	Satisfied	Neither satisfied nor dissatisfied	Dissatisfied	Very dissatisfied	No experience
☐	☐	☐	☐	☐	☐

Comments and suggestions for improvements:_____

_____

_____

_____

10. The way they keep you informed about IBM's products and services?

Very satisfied	Satisfied	Neither satisfied nor dissatisfied	Dissatisfied	Very dissatisfied	No experience
☐	☐	☐	☐	☐	☐

Comments and suggestions for improvements:_____

_____

_____

_____

11. The frequency of their contact to discuss IBM's products and services?

Very satisfied	Satisfied	Neither satisfied nor dissatisfied	Dissatisfied	Very dissatisfied	No experience
☐	☐	☐	☐	☐	☐

Comments and suggestions for improvements:_____

_____

_____

_____

Figure C.4 continued.

Products and Services

Software

12. How satisfied are you with:

	Very satisfied	Satisfied	Neither satisfied nor dissatisfied	Dissatisfied	Very dissatisfied	No experience
Their Application software?	☐	☐	☐	☐	☐	☐
The availability of appropriate Application software to run on the RISC System/6000?	☐	☐	☐	☐	☐	☐

Comments and suggestions for improvements:_____

_____
_____
_____

Technical support

Our Business Associate may provide you with post installation and "Hotline" support, offering guidance and assistance in managing your RISC System/6000.

13. How satisfied are you with this support?

Very satisfied	Satisfied	Neither satisfied nor dissatisfied	Dissatisfied	Very dissatisfied	No experience
☐	☐	☐	☐	☐	☐

Comments and suggestions for improvements:_____

_____
_____
_____

Education

Business Associates may provide a range of courses to help you use your RISC System/6000 effectively.

14. How satisfied are you with the education that you have received?

Very satisfied	Satisfied	Neither satisfied nor dissatisfied	Dissatisfied	Very dissatisfied	No experience
☐	☐	☐	☐	☐	☐

Comments and suggestions for improvements:_____

_____
_____
_____

Administrative support

15. How satisfied are you with our Business Associate's handling of your:

	Very satisfied	Satisfied	Neither satisfied nor dissatisfied	Dissatisfied	Very dissatisfied	No experience
Written communications?	☐	☐	☐	☐	☐	☐
Telephone communications?	☐	☐	☐	☐	☐	☐

Comments and suggestions for improvements:_____

_____
_____
_____

Figure C.4 continued.

IBM

The following questions refer to your satisfaction with IBM.

Products and services

Hardware

---

16. How satisfied are you with the following IBM hardware products?

	Very satisfied	Satisfied	Neither satisfied nor dissatisfied	Dissatisfied	Very dissatisfied	No experience
Processors	☐	☐	☐	☐	☐	☐
Disks	☐	☐	☐	☐	☐	☐
CDROM/Diskette/Tape	☐	☐	☐	☐	☐	☐
Printers	☐	☐	☐	☐	☐	☐
Displays	☐	☐	☐	☐	☐	☐

Comments and suggestions for improvements:

We would particularly welcome your comments in the areas of ease of use, reliability, function and documentation.

Product	Area	Comment
_____	_____	_____
_____	_____	_____
_____	_____	_____
_____	_____	_____
_____	_____	_____
_____	_____	_____
_____	_____	_____
_____	_____	_____

17. How satisfied are you with the IBM 'Open Options' catalogue?

Very satisfied	Satisfied	Neither satisfied nor dissatisfied	Dissatisfied	Very dissatisfied	No experience
☐	☐	☐	☐	☐	☐

Please consider range of third party products available, format etc.

Comments and suggestions for improvements:_____

_____

_____

_____

Figure C.4 continued.

Software

18. How satisfied are you with the following IBM software products?

	Very satisfied	Satisfied	Neither satisfied nor dissatisfied	Dissatisfied	Very dissatisfied	No experience
The AIX Operating system	☐	☐	☐	☐	☐	☐
Other IBM software (eg FORTRAN, AIX windows and AIX NetView)	☐	☐	☐	☐	☐	☐

Comments and suggestions for improvements:

We would particularly welcome your comments in the areas of ease of use, reliability, function and documentation.

Product	*Area*	*Comment*
_____	_____	_____
_____	_____	_____
_____	_____	_____
_____	_____	_____
_____	_____	_____

Maintenance

Your maintenance arrangements may involve IBM and/or your Business Associate (BA):

Please indicate the major source of maintenance for your IBM hardware.

- ☐ 1 IBM Maintenance contract
- ☐ 2 BA Maintenance contract, performed by IBM
- ☐ 3 BA Maintenance contract, performed by the BA
- ☐ 4 IBM Per Call
- ☐ 5 Other

If you have answered 5 above please go to question 21.

How satisfied are you with:

19. The speed of response to your hardware service calls (that is, from the time the problem is reported until the engineer starts to work on it)?

	Very satisfied	Satisfied	Neither satisfied nor dissatisfied	Dissatisfied	Very dissatisfied	No experience
	☐	☐	☐	☐	☐	☐
	☐	☐	☐	☐	☐	☐

Comments and suggestions for improvements:_____

_____
_____
_____

20. The hardware maintenance services provided by your engineer?

	Very satisfied	Satisfied	Neither satisfied nor dissatisfied	Dissatisfied	Very dissatisfied	No experience
	☐	☐	☐	☐	☐	☐
	☐	☐	☐	☐	☐	☐

Comments and suggestions for improvements:_____

_____
_____
_____

Figure C.4 continued.

Education
_ _

IBM Education Services can provide you with a wide spectrum of education and training, encompassing technical, personal and business skills.

21. How satisfied are you with the education
that you have received?

Very satisfied	Satisfied	Neither satisfied nor dissatisfied	Dissatisfied	Very dissatisfied	No experience
☐	☐	☐	☐	☐	☐

Comments and suggestions for improvements:_____

_____

_____

Administrative support
_ _

How satisfied are you with:

22. The quality of the maintenance
and support invoices you receive from IBM?

Very satisfied	Satisfied	Neither satisfied nor dissatisfied	Dissatisfied	Very dissatisfied	No experience
☐	☐	☐	☐	☐	☐

Comments and suggestions for improvements:_____

_____

_____

23. Our handling of your:

	Very satisfied	Satisfied	Neither satisfied nor dissatisfied	Dissatisfied	Very dissatisfied	No experience
Written communications?	☐	☐	☐	☐	☐	☐
Telephone communications?	☐	☐	☐	☐	☐	☐

Comments and suggestions for improvements:_____

_____

_____

24. The support you receive from administrative personnel?

Very satisfied	Satisfied	Neither satisfied nor dissatisfied	Dissatisfied	Very dissatisfied	No experience
☐	☐	☐	☐	☐	☐

Comments and suggestions for improvements:_____

_____

_____

Figure C.4 continued.

Summary

Please comment on what you consider to be the most NEGATIVE aspects of your dealings with IBM and your Business Associate.

IBM _____

_____

_____

_____

BUSINESS ASSOCIATE _____

_____

_____

_____

Please comment on what you consider to be the most POSITIVE aspects of your dealings with IBM and your Business Associate.

IBM _____

_____

_____

_____

BUSINESS ASSOCIATE _____

_____

_____

_____

Please tell us about any other topics that are important to you that you would like us to include in this questionnaire.

_____

_____

_____

_____

Please indicate the likelihood that you would choose IBM or your Business Associate as your supplier for these products and services, if you were deciding today.

	Definitely	Probably	Might or might not	Probably not	Definitely not
Total solution	☐	☐	☐	☐	☐
Hardware	☐	☐	☐	☐	☐
Application software	☐	☐	☐	☐	☐
Maintenance services	☐	☐	☐	☐	☐
Education	☐	☐	☐	☐	☐

If you are unlikely to choose us in any area it would help us to understand your reasons, thank you.

Product/service	Comment
_____	_____
_____	_____
_____	_____
_____	_____
_____	_____
_____	_____
_____	_____

Figure C.4 continued.

Importance

To help us to understand what is important to you, we would be grateful if you would indicate a rating against each of the following topics.

	Critical	Very important	Of some importance	Largely unimportant	Of no importance

IBM and your Business Associate

	Critical	Very important	Of some importance	Largely unimportant	Of no importance
Value from your investment	☐	☐	☐	☐	☐
Quality of products and services	☐	☐	☐	☐	☐
After sales support	☐	☐	☐	☐	☐

Your Business Associate

Understand your business	☐	☐	☐	☐	☐
Knowledge of RISC System/6000 range	☐	☐	☐	☐	☐
Combine products and services into solutions	☐	☐	☐	☐	☐
Information about products and services	☐	☐	☐	☐	☐
Frequency of contact	☐	☐	☐	☐	☐

Application software	☐	☐	☐	☐	☐
Availability of appropriate Application software	☐	☐	☐	☐	☐
Technical Support	☐	☐	☐	☐	☐
Education	☐	☐	☐	☐	☐

Written communications	☐	☐	☐	☐	☐
Telephone communications	☐	☐	☐	☐	☐

IBM

Quality of hardware	☐	☐	☐	☐	☐
'Open Options' catalogue	☐	☐	☐	☐	☐
Quality of Operating systems	☐	☐	☐	☐	☐
Quality of other software	☐	☐	☐	☐	☐

Speed of response to service calls	☐	☐	☐	☐	☐
Hardware maintenance services	☐	☐	☐	☐	☐

Education	☐	☐	☐	☐	☐

Quality of invoices	☐	☐	☐	☐	☐
Written communications	☐	☐	☐	☐	☐
Telephone communications	☐	☐	☐	☐	☐
Administrative personnel	☐	☐	☐	☐	☐

Figure C.4 continued.

Identity

_ _

Please complete the relevant sections below if you are not the individual to whom this survey was addressed or if the details of your organisation, as shown on the address label, are incorrect in any way.

NAME ——

TITLE ———

ORGANISATION ————————————————————————————————————

ADDRESS ——

———

———

———

———

If you do **not** wish the comments you have made to be passed to your IBM office and Business Associate for action, but prefer to remain anonymous, please tick the box below.

☐

Thank you for completing this questionnaire.

Please use the attached reply paid envelope to return it to:

GSR Group Ltd, 361-373 City Road, London, EC1V 1JJ, who have been commissioned by us to manage this survey.

Figure C.4 continued.

Appendix D

Delighting customer programme – business plan template

The template in Figure D.1 outlines the areas to be covered when developing a *Delighting Customers* business plan. In our experience the development of this document is essential to addressing strategic issues and the integration of the *Delighting Customers* programme into the business activities that drive the organization. The business plan would be updated on a quarterly basis and reviewed by the senior management team.

Template for delighting customer programme – business plan

Contents
1. Business case summary
2. Service vision, mission, objectives
3. Delighting customer's strategy
4. Targets: overall, markets, products and key accounts – customer satisfaction, employee satisfaction, market share and financials
5. Improvement project plans: owners and status – overall, markets, products and accounts
6. Communication plan: activities, status and customer impact
7. Major customer events
8. Results: current quarter, year to date, trending – overall, markets, products and accounts – customer satisfaction, employee satisfaction, market share and financials
9. Quarterly analysis report: successes, issues and recommendations

---

Figure D.1 Template for *Delighting Customer* programme – business plan.

Appendix E

Project management planning template

The template in Figure E.1 outlines the areas to be covered to manage effectively the improvement projects associated with becoming a customer-driven organization. We also include a set of 'quick-fix' solutions in Table E.1.

Template for customer satisfaction programme – project plan
(Oracle Corporation UK Limited)

Contents

Business case summary
1.   Issues and problem definition
2.   Objectives
3.   Scope
4.   Approach and timescales
5.   Team
6.   Budget
7.   Phase 2 work plan

   Step 1   Define issues and quantify business problems.
   Step 2   Analyse root causes.
   Step 3   Set targets for measuring success.
   Step 4   Define alternative solutions.
   Step 5   Decide implementation strategy for phase 3.
   Step 6   Prepare detailed implementation plan for phase 3.
   Step 7   Implementation, measurement and progress reporting.

   Appendix 1 Implementation strategy options

Figure E.1 Template for *Delighting Customers* programme project plan.
(*Source:* Oracle Corporation UK Limited)

Examples of 'quick-fixes' (Oracle Corporation UK Limited)

The solutions given in Table E.1 are actual examples taken from Oracle's customer satisfaction programme. The quick-fix project plan also includes columns for budget impact, timing and project manager, but these have been omitted from the examples given. The project column also includes the name of the sponsor, who may or may not be the same person as the project manager.

Table E.1 Examples of 'quick fixes'

Project	Problem	Solution	Objectives/ Benefits
The Oracle service proposition and values	Clarity of 'What does Oracle stand for?'	Develop and articulate to employees and customers	Direct the behaviour of individuals and the business planning process
Balanced scorecard for business planning	Narrow, introspective planning process	Include non-financial performance measures (customer satisfaction, employee satisfaction, continuous improvement)	Better manage the business. Establish early warning performance indicators.
Customer care training	No customer care training available	Commission training needs analysis, design programme, source supply	Raise employee awareness and drive specific improvements
Internal service levels	Internal services do not have a 'service driven' reputation as evidenced in the employee opinion survey	Each core internal service to define and measure key services provided	Improve service to front-line employees. Establish a service mentality throughout the organization.
Employee suggestion programme	Employees are a largely untapped source of service improvement ideas	An ongoing suggestion programme, triggered bi-annually	Improve customer satisfaction through specific, practical improvements

(*Source:* Oracle Corporation UK Limited)

Appendix F

Results reporting examples

The following result packs show an example of the approaches that organizations have taken to present effectively the findings from their customer feedback systems. The first example is taken from Northern Telecom's *Delighting Customers* programme and the second example is from IBM UK customer satisfaction programme. Details of the attribute descriptors – customers, products and markets – have been removed to maintain confidentiality of the results. This common format is used to present the results at company, business unit and account level. This common format facilitates the comparability of results across markets, products and accounts. Steps 6 (page 98) and 7 (page 112) cover this area in more detail.

RESULTS EXAMPLE

Northern Telecom Europe Ltd – *Delighting Customers* results pack is set out in Figures F.1–5 and Table F.1. Another set of results reporting is seen in the IBM United Kingdom Ltd – customer satisfaction result pack (see Figures F.6–F.9).

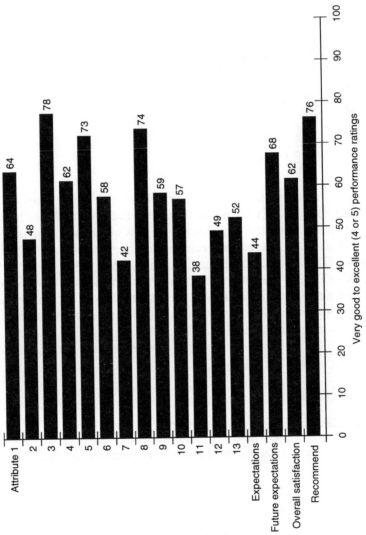

Figure F.1 Customer satisfaction performance – overall satisfaction.

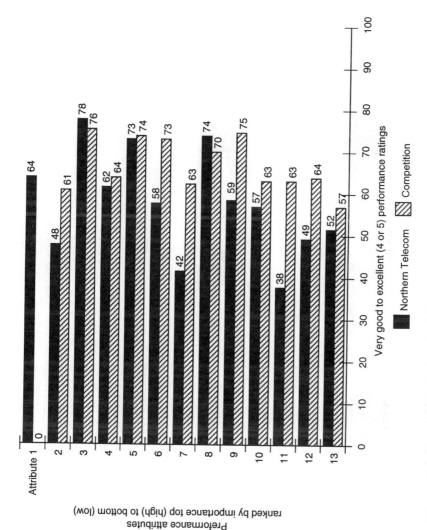

Figure F.2 Customer satisfaction performance – NT v. strongest competitor.

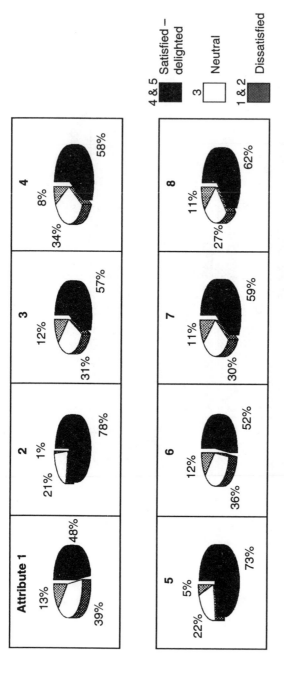

Figure F.3 Piechart format of customer satisfaction performance.

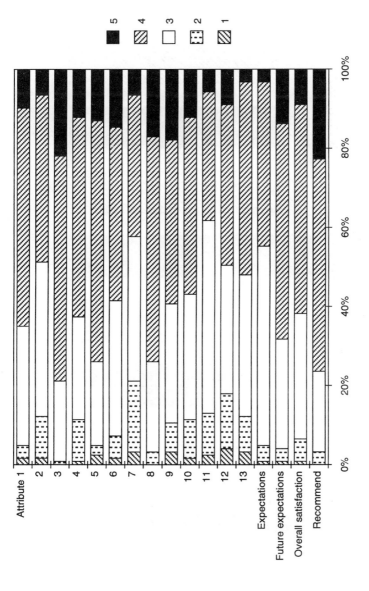

Figure F.4 Customer satisfaction performance – rating and distribution.

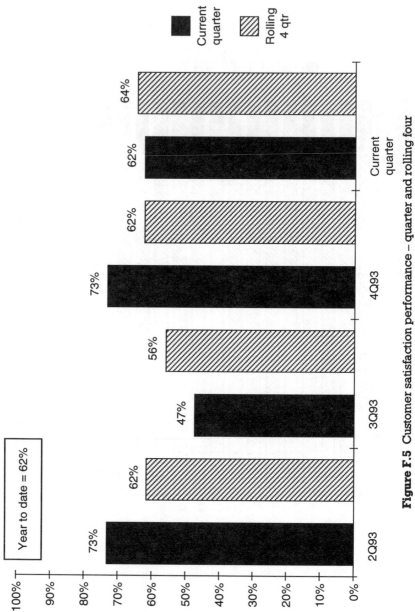

Figure F.5 Customer satisfaction performance – quarter and rolling four quarter result chart.

Table F.1 Customer satisfaction performance – shifts

	NT Performance				NT–CP (difference)		Competition		
	1994	1993	IR	94–93	1994	1993	1994	1993	94–93
Attribute 1	64	75	4.5	—11	64	75	0	0	0
Attribute 2	48	41	4.5	7	—13	—26	61	67	—6
Attribute 3	78	65	4.4	13	2	—13	76	78	—2
Attribute 4	62	42	4.4	20	—2	—22	64	64	0
Attribute 5	73	54	4.3	19	—1	—18	74	72	2
Attribute 6	58	52	4.3	6	—15	—1	73	53	20
Attribute 7	42	35	4.2	7	—21	—19	63	54	9
Attribute 8	74	59	4.2	15	4	—2	70	61	9
Attrubite 9	59	56	4.1	3	—16	—4	75	60	15
Attribute 10	57	63	4.1	—6	—6	—1	63	64	—1
Attribute 11	38	36	4.0	2	—25	—16	63	52	11
Attribute 12	49	63	3.9	—14	—15	—2	64	65	—1
Attribute 13	52	60	3.7	—8	—5	7	57	53	4
Expectations	44	48		—4					
Future Expectations	68	58		10					
Overall Satisfaction	62	44		18					
Recommend	76	66		10					
Base	210	91					163	80	

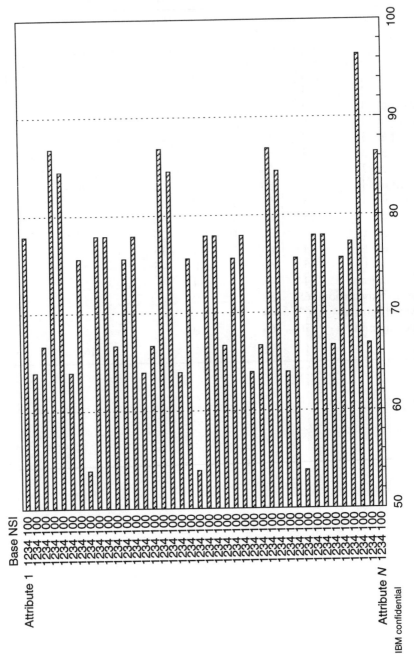

Figure F.6 NSI by question.

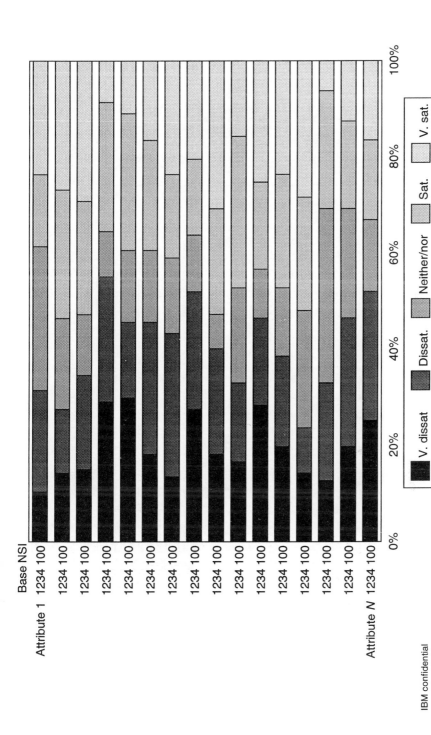

Figure F.7 Distribution scores – UK total.

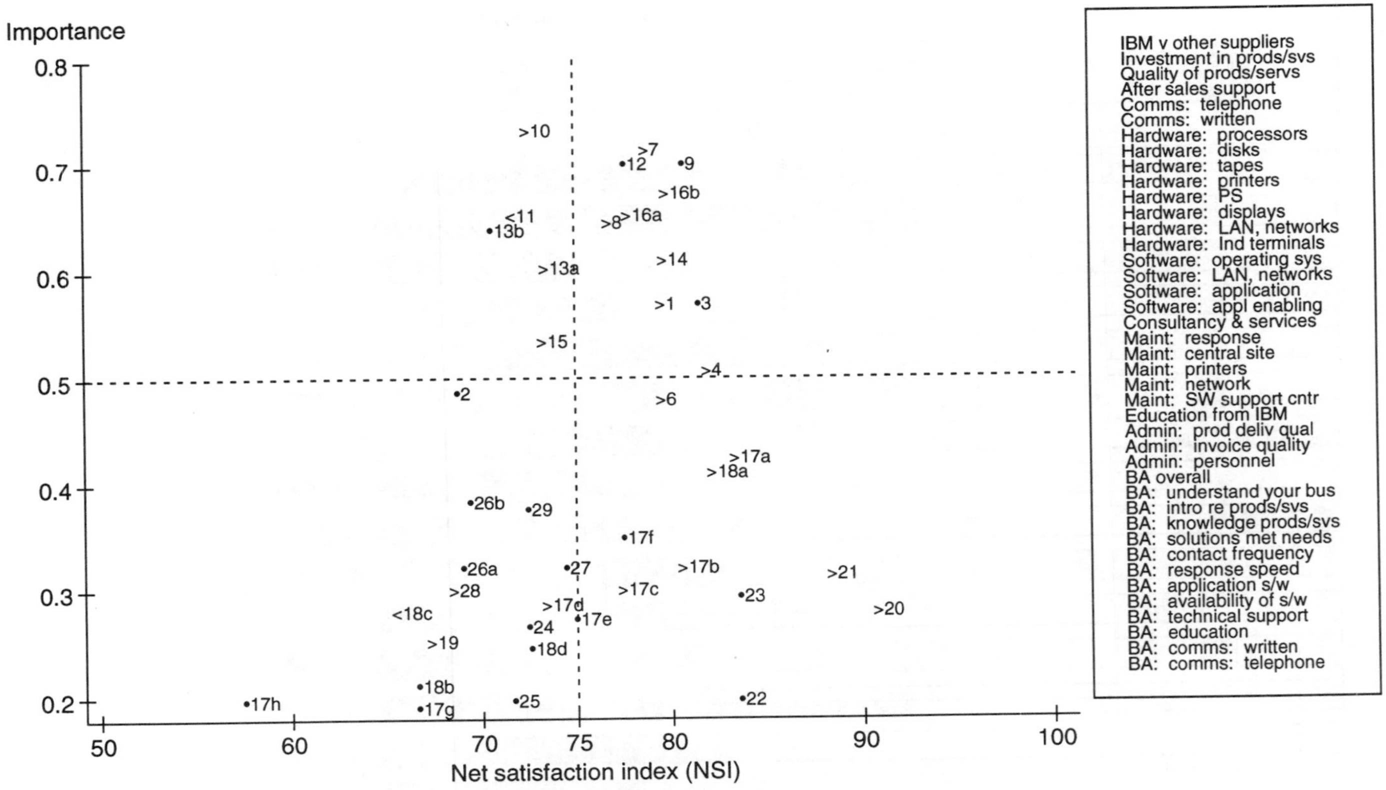
Importance
0.8
0.7
0.6
0.5
0.4
0.3
0.2
50
60
70
75
80
90
100
Net satisfaction index (NSI)
>10
>7
•12
•9
>16b
<11
•13b
>8
>16a
>14
>13a
>1
•3
>15
>4
•2
>6
>17a
>18a
•26b
•29
•17f
•26a
•27
>17b
>21
>28
>17c
•23
>20
<18c
>17d
•17e
•24
>19
•18d
•18b
•25
•22
•17h
•17g
IBM v other suppliers
Investment in prods/svs
Quality of prods/servs
After sales support
Comms: telephone
Comms: written
Hardware: processors
Hardware: disks
Hardware: tapes
Hardware: printers
Hardware: PS
Hardware: displays
Hardware: LAN, networks
Hardware: Ind terminals
Software: operating sys
Software: LAN, networks
Software: application
Software: appl enabling
Consultancy & services
Maint: response
Maint: central site
Maint: printers
Maint: network
Maint: SW support cntr
Education from IBM
Admin: prod deliv qual
Admin: invoice quality
Admin: personnel
BA overall
BA: understand your bus
BA: intro re prods/svs
BA: knowledge prods/svs
BA: solutions met needs
BA: contact frequency
BA: response speed
BA: application s/w
BA: availability of s/w
BA: technical support
BA: education
BA: comms: written
BA: comms: telephone

Figure F.8 Customer satisfaction/derived importance – UK total.

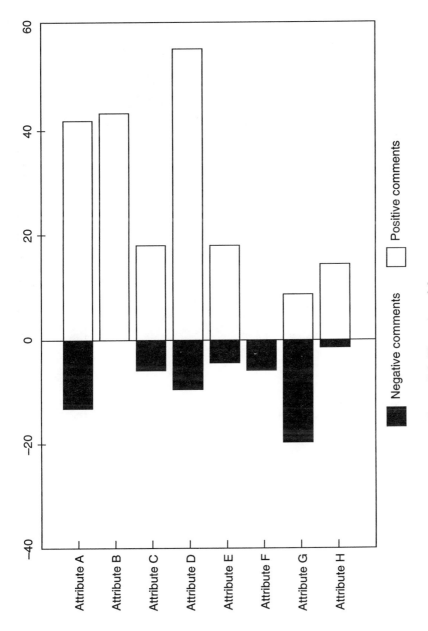

Figure F.9 The voice of the customer.

Appendix G

Communication plan template

Communication plays a significant part in *Delighting Customers* programmes. From the customer's viewpoint perception is everything. Customer perceptions change through what they hear (communications) and/or their experience of your products and services.

In the business-to-business environment, outside of operational performance, the gap between the customer's experience of your organization, products and services may be as long as 2–5 years. In these cases it is evident that an effective long-term communication programme is essential to enable them to form an up-to-date perception of your organization. Thus, when they decide to re-purchase or are asked for an opinion on your organization, they can form their opinion based on your current performance rather than on historical prejudices.

To gain the full benefits from your efforts you will need to communicate effectively the changes that you have made to address your customer's needs and expectations. The communications plan template (Figure G.1) outlines the activities to be covered in a *Delighting Customers* communication campaign.

Template for customer satisfaction communications plan

1. **Introduction**
   - Customers and markets
   - Products and services
   - Background
   - Communication needs and major issues
   - Business case

2. **Communications objectives**
   - Purpose
   - Target audiences (customer, employees and business community)

3. **Communications strategy**
   - Dedicated programmes for key messages
   - Development of communication channels and appropriate messages
   - Suggested areas to cover
     - Customers
     - Prospective customers, consultants and other opinion formers
     - Business partners, suppliers
     - The media – industry, business and key industry sector press
     - Investment community
     - Employees
   - Co-ordination with product and market business units

4. **Programme of activities**
   Suggested areas to be covered:
   - The programme of activities must convince people of the depth of commitment to the Delighting Customer's Programme and of its practical value to customers.
   - This will require a varied communications mix to reach the target audiences identified above.
   - Due to the specialist skills involved it is recommended that you use a communications consultancy to manage the implementation of this communications programme.

5. **Implementation plan**
   STEP 1 – preparation
   Suggested areas to cover:
   - Customer satisfaction story
   - Briefing document
   - Presentation material
   - Identification and preparation of spokespersons

Figure G.1 Template for *Delighting Customers* communications plan.

STEP 2 – set up communications channels and activities
Suggested areas to cover:

- Media channels
  - Internal magazine and publications
  - Internal promotional or speaking events
  - External promotional or speaking events
  - Leading national press – business and industry sector pages
  - UK, european and international dailies
  - Business management magazines – UK, european and international
  - Leading industry sector publications
- Customer endorsements
- Speaking engagements
- Advertising
- Customer satisfaction forums (key influencers from target audience groups)
- Co-ordination with other internal groups
- Customer satisfaction reports

STEP 3 – implementation plans
Suggested approach:

- Start with a few low key meetings (customer and employee) and speaking engagements. These events can be used to pilot the impact of the presentational material and then update as appropriate.
- Start to implement the other communication channels.
- Focus to be on a small list of top priority publications, and develop the customer endorsements for use in selected customer satisfaction forums and speaking engagements.
- Review the presentational material after feedback.
- Assess the effectiveness of each communication channel.
- Review the effectiveness of the communications channels.
- Utilise fully the communication channels that have the most effect.
- Co-ordinate activities with other internal groups.
- Utilise all the media channels.
- Identify the 'advertising message'.
- Communicate the successes widely through the customer satisfaction reports and customer satisfaction forums.

6. **Communications review**
   Suggested areas to cover:

   - Assess the effectiveness of the whole programme.
   - Include an assessment of the views of the target audiences – business community, customers and employees.

   As a minimum the measures of success should include:

   - increased awareness of the benefits of the programme by employees, customers and the business community;
   - increased customer loyalty; and
   - increased effectiveness of the customer satisfaction programme.

Figure G.1 continued.

Appendix H

European Foundation for Quality Management (EFQM) – customer satisfaction benchmarking questionnaire

During 1993 the European Foundation for Quality Management set up a customer satisfaction working group to develop a benchmarking survey.

The survey allows organizations to compare its *Delighting Customer* programme with others and to identify the key areas of interest and the processes to benchmark further. To develop the survey questionnaire the working group studied all available customer satisfactions models and used this information to identify the areas to be covered and the questions to ask.

The questionnaire was piloted on more than twenty organizations that were seen to be at the forefront of customer satisfaction. The results of the survey were reviewed with these organizations at a best practice day. The conclusion was that the benchmarking questionnaire covered all the essential areas and also provided an opportunity to identify future areas for comparision.

This questionnaire (see Figure H.1) can be used with a number of benchmarking partners or within your organization to get a feel for the strengths and weaknesses of your *Delighting Customer* programme and to identify specific areas for detailed benchmarking.

For further information contact the European foundation for Quality Management representative's office:

Avenue des Pléiades 19
B-1200 Brussels, Belgium
Tel.: +32 2 775 3511
Fax.: +32 2 775 3535

EFQM Customer Satisfaction Benchmarking Survey : 1993

The European Foundation for Quality Management

Name : _____
(optional)

Company : _____
(optional)

Function:
(please specify by ticking a box below)

Quality / Customer Service ☐
Finance ☐
Commercial (Sales / Marketing) ☐
Personnel / Human Resources ☐
Distribution / Logistics ☐
Other (please state) _____ ☐

Guidelines and Areas to be Measured

This questionnaire will measure the characteristics
and performance of your company in the areas shown
opposite.

All answers in this questionnaire will be treated in
complete confidence and will be used only by the
persons engaged in the survey.

For each question, please indicate the answer
(or answers) by ticking the corresponding box(es),
e.g. ☑ or by writing in the answer.

Please ensure that your questionnaire is returned
to The Chairman of the EFQM Customer Satisfaction
Working Group:

Mr. Peter Donovan
Customer Satisfaction Manager
Northern Telecom Europe Ltd
Stafferton Way
Maidenhead
Berkshire SL6 1AY England

Tel: 0628 812170
Fax: 0628 812180

Culture

Customer Satisfaction Policy

Customer Involvement

Communications

Organisation and People Involvement

Impact on Performance

Measuring Customer Satisfaction

General Questions

This survey is designed to compare the characteristics and performance of EFQM member companies in delivering products and
services that fully satisfy the needs and expectations of their customers. The EFQM Customer Satisfaction Working Group
studied all available models on Customer Satisfaction and from this information they designed the Benchmarking Survey. The
survey has been carried out on 20 member companies who were seen as being at the forefront of customer satisfaction. The
results of the survey , question set, and survey methodology was reviewed with this group at a Best Practice day . The
conclusion was that the Benchmarking Survey covered all the key areas and also provided the opportunity to identify future areas
for comparison. Further information on the results and conclusions can be obtained from the EFQM office in Brussels.

CSTF /   /   /   /   /

Figure H.1 The EFQM questionnaire.

1. Culture and Customer Satisfaction Policy

1A. Does your company have a documented Customer Satisfaction Policy / Mission Statement ?

Yes ☐ Go to Q1B

No ☐
Don't Know ☐
Not Applicable ☐ Go to Q1D

1B. If yes, to whom is it communicated ?
Tick as appropriate

a. Board Members ☐
b. Senior Management ☐
c. Middle Management ☐
d. Lower management ☐
e. All Employees ☐

1C. How is it communicated ?
Tick as appropriate

a. Through reviews / seminars ☐
b. On notice boards ☐
c. By letter / memorandum ☐
d. Other (please state) _____ ☐

1D. Is your company actively involved in improving Customer Satisfaction ?

Yes ☐ Go to Q1E

No ☐
Don't Know ☐
Not Applicable ☐ Go to Q1F

1E. If yes, please indicate why ?
Tick as appropriate

a. To increase customer loyalty ☐
b. To improve company image ☐
c. To increase company productivity ☐
d. To increase company efficiency ☐
e. To enhance the company's reputation ☐
f. To reduce customer turnover ☐
g. To reduce employee turnover ☐
h. To improve business performance ☐
i. Other (please state) _____

_____

Figure H.1 continued.

1. Culture and Customer Satisfaction Policy (continued)

1F. Does your company have a Customer Care
standard in terms of service performance
and / or guarantees ?

Yes ☐ Go to Q1G

No ☐
Don't Know ☐
Not Applicable ☐ Go to Q1I

1G. If yes, do you measure your performance against
these standards ?

Yes ☐ Go to Q1H

No ☐
Don't Know ☐
Not Applicable ☐ Go to Q1I

1H. If yes, please state how ?

_____

_____

_____

1I. Considering your company's **culture** on Customer satisfaction, on an overall
basis, how would you rate the statements below using the following scale:
Where 1 = Totally disagree, 2 = Mainly disagree, 3 = Neither agree nor disagree,
4 = Mainly agree, 5 = Fully agree.

1 2 3 4 5

a. Our company has an effective Customer Satisfaction policy   ☐ ☐ ☐ ☐ ☐

b. Our company has clearly defined the Product / Service
quality to be provided to its customers   ☐ ☐ ☐ ☐ ☐

c. Our company sets targets and defines the necessary objectives   ☐ ☐ ☐ ☐ ☐
to increase Customer Satisfaction

d. Our company monitors Customer Satisfaction on a regular basis ☐ ☐ ☐ ☐ ☐

e. Our company continually implements Customer Satisfaction
improvements   ☐ ☐ ☐ ☐ ☐

f. Senior Managers are aware of Customer Satisfaction rates   ☐ ☐ ☐ ☐ ☐

g. All employees are aware of Customer Satisfaction rates   ☐ ☐ ☐ ☐ ☐

h. Senior Managers are actively involved in the implementation
of Customer Satisfaction improvements   ☐ ☐ ☐ ☐ ☐

i. Our company's Customer Satisfaction rates increase each year   ☐ ☐ ☐ ☐ ☐

Figure H.1 continued.

2. Customer Involvement

Considering your company's approach to **customer involvement** on an overall basis, how would you rate the statements below using the following scale:
Where 1 = Totally disagree, 2 = Mainly disagree, 3 = Neither agree nor disagree, 4 = Mainly agree, 5 = Fully agree.

	1	2	3	4	5
a. Customer Satisfaction performances, against set standards and / or guarantees, are regularly reviewed with customers	□	□	□	□	□
b. Customers are strongly encouraged to make comments and suggestions for improvements	□	□	□	□	□
c. Our company fully understands our customers' business practises, procedures and business goals	□	□	□	□	□
e. Advanced methods such as Quality Function Deployment are used to capture customer requirements	□	□	□	□	□

Considering your company's approach to **customer contact** on an overall basis, how would you rate the statements below using the following scale:
Where 1 = Totally disagree, 2 = Mainly disagree, 3 = Neither agree nor disagree, 4 = Mainly agree, 5 = Fully agree.

	1	2	3	4	5
f. Our customers regularly communicate with our Quality / Customer Service department	□	□	□	□	□
g. Our customers regularly communicate with our Operations / Distribution and Logistics department	□	□	□	□	□
h. Our customers regularly communicate with our Senior Managers	□	□	□	□	□
i. Our customers regularly communicate with our Research and Development department	□	□	□	□	□
j. Our customers regularly communicate with our Sales department	□	□	□	□	□
k. Our customers regularly communicate with our Marketing department	□	□	□	□	□
l. Our customers regularly communicate with our Finance / Accounts department	□	□	□	□	□

Figure H.1 continued.

3. Communications

Considering your company's approach to **customer communications**, on an overall basis, how would you rate the statements below using the following scale: Where 1 = Totally disagree, 2 = Mainly disagree, 3 = Neither agree nor disagree, 4 = Mainly agree, 5 = Fully agree.

	1	2	3	4	5
a. Our customers fully understand the products and services provided by our company	□	□	□	□	□
b. Our company provides accurate order-status information to our customers	□	□	□	□	□
c. Our customers are kept informed on how their problems are being tackled	□	□	□	□	□
d. Our customers know who to call or write to if they have a complaint	□	□	□	□	□
e. Our customers fully understand our complaints procedure	□	□	□	□	□

Considering your company's approach to **employee communications**, on an overall basis, how would you rate the statements below using the following scale: Where 1 = Totally disagree, 2 = Mainly disagree, 3 = Neither agree nor disagree, 4 = Mainly agree, 5 = Fully agree.

	1	2	3	4	5
f. Our employees fully understand the concerns of our customers	□	□	□	□	□
g. Our employees fully understand the company's procedure for handling customer complaints	□	□	□	□	□
h. Our employees are aware of the service standards and guarantees offered to our customers.	□	□	□	□	□
i. Our employees are aware of how our customers use our products and services	□	□	□	□	□
j. Our Company has a formal process for disseminating information and policy to its employees	□	□	□	□	□

Figure H.1 continued.

4. Organisation and People Involvement

Considering your company's **organisation and the way it involves its people**, on an overall basis, how would you rate the statements below using the following scale: Where 1 = Totally disagree, 2 = Mainly disagree, 3 = Neither agree nor disagree, 4 = Mainly agree, 5 = Fully agree.

                1 2 3 4 5

a. The organisational structure of our company makes it easy for customers to get accurate answers and timely actions in response to their enquiries or complaints □ □ □ □ □

b. All customers' remarks, questions and problems are traceable within our company □ □ □ □ □

c. Our front-line people are empowered to take actions and solve problems for customers when needed □ □ □ □ □

d. Our managers are evaluated and rewarded according to customer satisfaction improvements □ □ □ □ □

e. Our company rewards people for thinking long term and working to retain customers □ □ □ □ □

f. Specific training is provided to people to assure consistent customer service □ □ □ □ □

g. The main **strength** of our organisation and the way in which we involve our people is -
(please state below)

_____

_____

_____

_____

h. The main **improvement opportunity** for our company's organisation and the way in which we involve our people is -
(please state below)

_____

_____

_____

_____

Figure H.1 continued.

5. Customer Satisfaction Impact on Performance

Considering the **impact** that Customer Satisfaction has **on your company's performance**, on an overall basis, how would you rate the statements below using the following scale: Where 1 = Totally disagree, 2 = Mainly disagree, 3 = Neither agree nor disagree, 4 = Mainly agree, 5 = Fully agree.

		1	2	3	4	5
a.	We evaluate the costs of losing a customer	☐	☐	☐	☐	☐
b.	We evaluate the cost of maintaining a customer	☐	☐	☐	☐	☐
c.	We evaluate the cost of solving customer problems	☐	☐	☐	☐	☐
d.	We evaluate the cost of acquiring a new customer	☐	☐	☐	☐	☐
e.	We evaluate the effect that our Customer Satisfaction Programme has on our performance	☐	☐	☐	☐	☐
f.	We evaluate the effect that customer complaint rates have on our performance	☐	☐	☐	☐	☐

g. The main **strength** of the way in which our company uses
   Customer Satisfaction to impact its performance is
   (please state below)

   _____

   _____

   _____

   _____

h. The main **improvement opportunity** for the way in which our
   company uses Customer Satisfaction to impact its performance is -
   (please state below)

   _____

   _____

   _____

   _____

Figure H.1 continued.

6. Measuring Customer Satisfaction

Our company undertakes the following types of surveys:
(please specify by ticking the boxes below)

a. Customer Satisfaction   Yes ☐   No ☐

If yes, please indicate frequency and research methods

once a year ☐   several times a year ☐   other (please state)_____

mailed questionnaires ☐   telephone interviews ☐   personal interviews ☐

focus groups ☐   comment cards ☐   other (please state)_____

b. Company image   Yes ☐   No ☐

If yes, please indicate frequency and research methods

once a year ☐   several times a year ☐   other (please state)_____

mailed questionnaires ☐   telephone interviews ☐   personal interviews ☐

focus groups ☐   comment cards ☐   other (please state)_____

c.   Lost Customers   Yes ☐   No ☐

If yes, please indicate frequency and research methods

once a year ☐   several times a year ☐   other (please state)_____

mailed questionnaires ☐   telephone interviews ☐   personal interviews ☐

focus groups ☐   comment cards ☐   other (please state)_____

d. Competitive   Yes ☐   No ☐

If yes, please indicate frequency and research methods

once a year ☐   several times a year ☐   other (please state)_____

mailed questionnaires ☐   telephone interviews ☐   personal interviews ☐

focus groups ☐   comment cards ☐   other (please state)_____

Figure H.1 continued.

6. Measuring Customer Satisfaction (continued)

Our company undertakes the following types of surveys:
(please specify by ticking the boxes below)

e. **Potential Customers**   Yes ☐   No ☐

If yes, please indicate frequency and research methods

once a year ☐   several times a year ☐   other (please state)_____

mailed questionnaires ☐   telephone interviews ☐   personal interviews ☐

focus groups ☐   comment cards ☐   other (please state)_____

f. **Employee Satisfaction**   Yes ☐   No ☐

If yes, please indicate frequency and research methods

once a year ☐   several times a year ☐   other (please state)_____

mailed questionnaires ☐   telephone interviews ☐   personal interviews ☐

focus groups ☐   comment cards ☐   other (please state)_____

g. **Others (please state type)**_____

Please indicate frequency and research methods

once a year ☐   several times a year ☐   other (please state)_____

mailed questionnaires ☐   telephone interviews ☐   personal interviews ☐

focus groups ☐   comment cards ☐   other (please state)_____

h. **Others (please state type)**_____

Please indicate frequency and research methods

once a year ☐   several times a year ☐   other (please state)_____

mailed questionnaires ☐   telephone interviews ☐   personal interviews ☐

focus groups ☐   comment cards ☐   other (please state)_____

Figure H.1 continued.

7. General Questions - about your company

Considering the **characteristics and performance of your company in fully meeting the needs and expectations of your customers,** how would you rate the statements below using the following scale: Where 1 = Totally disagree, 2 = Mainly disagree, 3 = Neither agree nor disagree, 4 = Mainly agree, 5 = Fully agree.

                                                1   2   3   4   5

a. A Customer focused culture is a major strength of our company ☐ ☐ ☐ ☐ ☐

b. Our Customer Satisfaction policy is a major strength of our company ☐ ☐ ☐ ☐ ☐

c. The way that we involve our customers is a major strength of our company ☐ ☐ ☐ ☐ ☐

d. The way in which we communicate internally and externally is a major strength of our company ☐ ☐ ☐ ☐ ☐

e. The way in which we organise and involve our people is a major strength of our company ☐ ☐ ☐ ☐ ☐

f. The way in which our Customer Satisfaction Programme impacts on our performance is a major strength of our company ☐ ☐ ☐ ☐ ☐

g. The effectiveness of our Customer Satisfaction Measurement programme is a major strength of our company ☐ ☐ ☐ ☐ ☐

h. The **other major strengths** displayed by our company in fully meeting the needs and expectations of our customers are - (please state below)

_____

_____

_____

I. The **main improvement opportunities** for our company in fully meeting the needs and expectations of our customers are - (please state below)

_____

_____

_____

Figure H.1 continued.

8. General Questions - about this questionnaire

Considering the **characteristics chosen in this questionnaire to measure Customer Satisfaction** performance, how would you rate the statements below using the following scale: Where 1 = Totally disagree, 2 = Mainly disagree, 3 = Neither agree nor disagree, 4 = Mainly agree, 5 = Fully agree.

1 2 3 4 5

a. A customer focused Culture is a key characteristic of companies that fully satisfy their customers' needs and expectations   □ □ □ □ □

b. Companies that fully satisfy their customers' needs and expectations should have a Customer Satisfaction Policy   □ □ □ □ □

c. Effective internal and external communications is a key characteristic of companies that fully satisfy their customers' needs and expectations   □ □ □ □ □

d. Companies that fully satisfy their customers' needs and expectations have an organisation tailored towards the way their customers do business.   □ □ □ □ □

e. Companies that fully satisfy their customers' needs and expectations involve all of their people in satisfying the customer   □ □ □ □ □

f. Having an effective Customer Satisfaction Measurement system is a key characteristic of those companies that fully satisfy their customers' needs and expectations   □ □ □ □ □

g. Are there **any other characteristics**, not covered by the survey, that you feel are essential to ensuring that companies fully satisfy their customers' needs and expectations   Yes □   No □

If yes, please note below

_____

_____

_____

_____

_____

_____

_____

Figure H.1 continued.

8. General Questions - about this questionnaire (continued)

Considering the **questions asked under each of the sections** in this questionnaire, how would you rate the statements below using the following scale:
Where 1 = Totally disagree, 2 = Mainly disagree, 3 = Neither agree nor disagree, 4 = Mainly agree, 5 = Fully agree.

	1	2	3	4	5
h. The questions asked in section 1 capture the key areas associated with Culture and Customer Satisfaction Policy	☐	☐	☐	☐	☐
i. The questions asked in section 2 capture the key areas associated with Customer Involvement	☐	☐	☐	☐	☐
j. The questions asked in section 3 capture the key areas associated with Communications	☐	☐	☐	☐	☐
k. The questions asked in section 4 capture the key areas associated with Organisation and People Involvement	☐	☐	☐	☐	☐
l. The questions asked in section 5 capture the key areas associated with Impact on Performance	☐	☐	☐	☐	☐
m. The questions asked in section 6 capture the key areas associated with Measuring Customer Satisfaction	☐	☐	☐	☐	☐

n . Are there **any other questions**, not covered by the survey, that you feel should be included to capture the characteristics and performance of companies that fully satisfy their customers' needs and expectations   Yes ☐   No ☐

If yes, please note below

_____

_____

_____

_____

_____

_____

_____

_____

END OF QUESTIONNAIRE - THANK YOU FOR PARTICIPATING IN THIS SURVEY

Figure H.1 continued.

Appendix I

Further reading

INTRODUCTION

This book has been based on our broad experiences within business and the development and successful implementation of our own *Delighitng Customer* programmes. We have been involved in several best practice studies and have debated this area and our secrets of success with many practitioners and senior executives around the world. We have also read widely in and around the field of *Delighting Customers*. The following list represents our suggestions for further reading.

FURTHER READING

Albrecht, K. and Bradford, L.J. (1990) *The Service Advantage – How to Identify and Fulfill Customer Needs*, Dow Jones-Irwin, Illinois.

Argyris, C. (1977) Double loop learning in organizations. *Harvard Business Review,* Sept–Oct.

Bennis, W. and Nanus, B. (1985) *Leaders,* Harpers & Row, New York.

Berry, L.L. (1980) Services marketing is different. *Business Magazine,* **24**, May–June, 24–9.

Berry, L.L. and Parasuraman, A. (1991) *Marketing Services – Competing Through Quality,* The Free Press, New York.

Berry, L.L., Zeithaml, V.A. and Parasuraman, A. (1985) Quality counts in services too. *Business Horizons,* May–June, 44–52.

Bitner, M.J. Nyquist, J.D. and Booms, B.H. (1985) The critical incident as a technique for analyzing the service encounter, in (eds T.M. Bloch, G.D Upah and V.A. Zeithaml) *Services Marketing in a Changing Environment,* American Marketing Association, Chigago.

Booms, B.H. and Bitner, M.J. (1981) Marketing strategies and organization structures for service firms, in *Marketing of Services:*

1981 (eds J. Donnelly and W. George) Special Conference Proceedings, American Marketing Association, Chicago.

Brouwer, P.J. (1964) The power to see ourselves, *Harvard Business Review* November–December Number 64602.

Camp, R.C. (1989) *Benchmarking – The Search for Industry Best Practices that Lead to Superior Performance,* ASQC Quality Press, Wisconsin.

Carlzon, J. (1987) *Moments of Truth,* Ballinger Cambridge, Massachusetts.

Deming, W.E. (1986) *Out of the Crisis,* MIT CAES, Cambridge, Massachusetts.

Gale, T.B., (1994) *Managing Customer Value,* The Free Press.

Garvin, D.A. (1993) Building a learning organization. *Harvard Business Review,* **71**(4) 78–91.

Gronroos, C. (1990) *Service Management and Marketing: Managing the Moments of Truth in Service Competition,* Lexington Books, Lexington, Massachusetts.

Handy, C. (1990) *The Age of Unreason,* Harvard Business Schoool Press, Boston Massachusetts.

Herzberg, F. (1968) One more time: how do you motivate employees? *Harvard Business Review,* January–February, Number 68108.

Heskett, J.L. (1987) Lessons in service sector. *Harvard Business Review,* **65**(2), 118–26.

Heskett, J.L., Earl Sasser, W. Jr, Hart, C.W.L. (1990) *Service Breakthroughs,* The Free Press, New York.

Juran, J.M. (1982) *Upper Management and Quality,* Juran Institute, Inc., New York.

Lash, L.M. (1989) *The Complete Guide to Customer Service,* John Wiley & Sons, New York.

Levitt, T. (1975) Marketing myopia. *Harvard Business Review,* September–October Number 75507.

Levitt, T. (1981) Marketing intangible products and product intangibles. *Harvard Business Review,* **59**(3) 94–102.

Livingston, J.S. (1971) Myth of the well-educated manager. *Harvard Business Review,* January–February Number 71108.

Lynch, J.J. (1992) *The Psychology of Customer Care,* The Macmillan Press Limited, London.

McKenna, R. (1992) *Relationship Marketing,* Century Business, London.

McNealy, R.M. (1994) *Making Customer Satisfaction Happen,* Chapman & Hall, London.

Morgan G. (1986) *Images of Organization,* Sage Publications Ltd, London.

Normann, R. and Ramirez, R. (1993) From value chain to value constellation: designing interactive strategy. *Harvard Business Review,* **71**(4), 65–77.

Parasuraman, A., Berry, L.L. and Zeithaml, V.A. (1991) Understanding customer expectations of service. *Sloan Management Review,* Spring, 39–48.

Paul, W.J. Jr, Robertson, K.B. and Herzberg, F. (1969) Job enrichment pays off. *Harvard Business Review,* March–April, Number 69209.

Peters, T. (1992) *Liberation Management,* Macmillan, London.

Quinn, J.B., Doorley, T.L. and Paquette, P.C. (1990) Beyond products: services-based strategy. *Harvard Business Review,* March–April, 58–67.

Rogers, C.R. and Roethlisberger, F.J. (1952) Barriers and gateways to communication. *Harvard Business Review* July–August, Number 52408.

Senge, P.M. (1990) *The Fifth Discipline: The Art and Practice of The Learning Organization,* Century Business/Random House, London.

Sewell, C. and Brown, P.B. (1991) *The Golden Rules of Customer Care,* Business Books Limited, London.

Seymour, D.T. (1988) *Marketing Research. Qualitative Methods for the Marketing Professional,* Probus Publishing Company, Chicago.

Soloman, M.R., Surprenant, C.F., Czepiel, J.A. and Gutman, E.G. (1985) A role theory perspective on dyadic interactions: the service encounter. *Journal of marketing,* **49**(1), 99–111.

Stata, R. (1989) Organizational learning: the key to management innovation. *Sloan Management Review,* Spring.

Surprenant, C.F. and Solomon, M.R. (1987) Predicatability and personalization in the service encounter. *Journal of Marketing,* **51**(2), 86–9.

Tannenbaum R. and Schmidt, W.H. (1973) How to choose a leadership pattern. *Harvard Business Review,* May–June, Number 73311.

Wee, C.H., Lee, K.S. and Hidajat, B.W. (1991) *Sun Tzu: War & Management,* Addison-Wesley Publishing Co., Inc., Singapore.

Whiteley, R.C. (1991) *The Customer Driven Company,* Business Books Limited, London.

Zeithaml, V.A. Parasuraman, A. and Berry, L.L. (1985) Problems and strategies in service marketing. *Journal of Marketing,* **49**(2), 33–46.

Index